GOD S LET THERE AND THERE WAS "LLUMO"

TRANSITIONING FROM APOLLO 11
MISSION CONTROL TO COMBAT
IN VIETNAM AND HEALING THE SCARS OF WAR

Ray W. Luce

outskirts
press

Table of Contents

Dedication and Gratitude

THIS BOOK IS dedicated to my wonderful son, Bryan Edward Luce. I'm very proud of him. Like his father, Bryan is an Eagle Scout. Also, Bryan worked diligently to earn an engineering degree from the University of Texas in Austin, and a master of business administration degree from Rice University in Houston. He's had a successful business career, and many business successes lie ahead. His smile is infectious, and he relates to people from all walks of life. I wish him many years of happiness.

I owe many debts of gratitude for the wonderful life I have enjoyed and the experiences I have known, good and bad, that led to this book:

- First and foremost, I want to thank my beautiful bride of almost forty years, Anita Coci Luce. She has been there for me during many of the events recounted in this book.
- I must thank my younger brother, Kenneth Allen Luce, for his lifelong friendship. He's an accomplished, recognized Houston artist. I was never a match for Kenneth's creativity. This book is probably as close as I will ever get.

- I want to thank the men of the 2nd Battalion (mechanized) 47th Infantry Regiment who I served with in Vietnam. From them, I learned the strength of a brotherhood no force can break, not even an opposing army.

- I want to thank Colonel Brice H. Barnes, a highly decorated army officer who served in the 2nd Battalion (mechanized) 47th Infantry Regiment. Colonel Barnes was in the 47th a couple of years before I arrived, but returned to Vietnam and, in a different unit, was in Cambodia while I was there in 1970. Colonel Barnes encouraged me to write this book. I recommend his book, *Vignettes from Vietnam*, which is available on Amazon.

- For my professional career, I must thank Dave Hilfman, Senior Vice President Worldwide Sales for Continental Airlines and, after the merger, United Airlines. Thanks to Dave, I enjoyed a great career as the sales attorney for Continental and United. I was fortunate to be able to travel the world for business and enjoyed every minute.

- Finally, I want to thank my buddy, Ron Blaylock, for years of fun and friendship. Mardi Gras in New Orleans wouldn't be the same without him.

A Note on the Cover

THE 2ND BATTALION (mechanized) 47th Infantry Regiment 9th Division spent almost three months on its trek through Vietnam, into Cambodia, and back into Vietnam. Those were three very difficult months of hardship and fighting. Many of us were mindeful of our unit mottos. The motto of the 2nd Battalion was "Panthers never quit." We were Panthers. The motto of the 47th Infantry Regiment was "Ex Virtute Honos" (Honor comes from virtue.). During the Cambodian campaign, the 2nd Battalion suffered seventy-eight casualties: twelve killed and sixty-six wounded, a twenty percent casualty rate. Eventually, we were back in some of our previous base camps and our officers finally had the time to recognize their troops with awards. I ended up back in Tan An, headquarters for the 9th Division, about fifty miles south of Saigon. In the picture on the cover, I, Ray W. Luce, am being awarded the Army Commendation Medal for "exceptionally meritorious achievement in support of military operations against communist aggression in the Republic of Vietnam."

My Army Commendation Medal was not awarded for valor, and I don't believe I did anything particularly valorous. I will tell you that, during those three months, in and out of Cambodia, one day I was working with my napalm unit, the Flame Platoon. Our army engineers were working on a stretch of dirt road. It was obvious where the road was going. So, at night, the VC would plant mines. Each morning for a few days the Flame Platoon laid out ribbons of flaming napalm where the road work was to occur. The hot flames detonated the mines and made it safe for the engineers to work. On both sides of the road, it was wet and marshy. One day a couple of mortar rounds came in and landed in the marshy ground on each side of the road. I was standing on top of my truck mixing two hundred gallons of napalm in my mix pot. I was splattered with mud when the mortars hit. Luckily, the shrapnel missed me. But I stood my post. A flame track was on the way back for refill and my job was to deliver. Not valorous—just another day at work fighting a war.

If you study the cover carefully, you will notice a background image of five armored personnel carriers entering the wood line of an abandoned rubber plantation. For a clearer look at the picture, it's included in chapter 3, "The Army," under "The Reluctant Tunnel Rat" vignette. I took this picture from the cab of my truck. As it turned out, we were stalled in the paddies because, maybe a half mile ahead of us, in the rubber, our convoy was ambushed. We were stuck for a couple of hours while that element of the convoy fought it out. A propeller driven spotter plane came in firing aiming rockets into the rubber. A couple of F4 Phantom jets followed, screaming in right over me and firing lethal rockets. The power of those jets and their rockets was bone shaking. Stuck in the paddies, outside the rubber, we could do nothing but wait. Finally, the fight was over, and the column moved through the ambush area into our RON (remain overnight) site. Passed a burned out armored personnel carrier. We circled in the RON as it was getting dark and, shortly thereafter, our perimeter was probed. So, a mad minute of amazing firepower ensued; thousands of tracer rounds spraying out. Officers were running around shouting "Check fire.", "Check fire." But one of our sergeants shouted, "The hell with check fire.", and launched a red flare. As long as a red flare was in the air, no way anyone would cease fire. All in all, an adrenalin rush you can't imagine.

Preface

FOLLOWING IS A self-reflective explanation of how I came to write this book.

After World War II, there were several crucial events that greatly affected the nation. The underlying event was creation of the unparalleled national prosperity achieved during the last half of the twentieth century. A second event, which launched simultaneously, was the advent of the baby boomer generation, and the astounding prosperity permitted the baby boomers to grow up experiencing the most comfortable physical conditions ever achieved in our country's history. The third event, and I believe the most spiritually spectacular, was the baby boomers, their parents, and their grandparents witnessing the US space program established, evolve, and, ultimately, achieve man's greatest technological achievement, Apollo 11's landing on the moon. The nation's reaction to that unfolding challenge and ultimate success was uplifting beyond most understanding, possibly in some sense approaching the metaphysical. The final event, which unfolded concurrently with the others, was the Vietnam War. Of these contemporary events, the Vietnam War was so antithetical to the others as to create, at the least, a subliminal dichotomy in the psyche of the nation.

The foregoing analysis addresses the nation as an aggregate, but national aggregates are composed of individual elements, its citizens. Therefore, the national dichotomy described above was resident, to differing degrees, in its individual citizens. The baby boomers who were called to fight in Vietnam were most affected. They experienced the dichotomy in both physical and mental reality: third world poverty versus prosperity, hardship versus comfort, and the hard realities of war versus unprecedented intellectual and technological achievements. I was affected in a unique way.

I worked in the US space program at the Manned Spacecraft Center (MSC) in Houston as a protocol officer. I worked there three years during the last five Gemini missions and all the Apollo missions through Apollo 11. My job was handling all MSC visitors including nontechnical, technical, and VIP. I was in mission control for all the foregoing missions including Apollo 11. I received my draft notice during Apollo 11. Seven months later I was carrying an M16 in Vietnam. I was a twenty-three-year-old college graduate when I arrived in Vietnam on February 26, 1970, and the first day I began asking myself "Where am I?" After I left Vietnam on April 13, 1971, I began asking myself "Where was I?" I never suffered any PTSD, but the answers to those questions haunted me over the ensuing years. In search of the answers, I began to write elements of this book during the early nineties.

Having attempted to explain why I wrote this book, allow me to suggest how to approach it. The book is essentially an autobiographical anthology composed of vignettes in chronological order. I recommend reading the book straight through to appreciate the evolution of my experiences and thinking, but each vignette is purposefully self-contained. So, feel free to read any vignette independently. But please note that because the vignettes are independent there is some repetition in describing certain settings where the events described occurred in the same place and during the same general time frame.

In chapter 1, "The Formative Years," you will notice references to Milby and Milby Buffalos. Lest you be perplexed, I attended Milby High School in Houston and we were Buffalos. Also, in chapter 4, "Letters Home from the Front," I should explain why I selected those letters. I was in Vietnam and Cambodia fourteen months. I wrote home often. So, I have well over a hundred letters that my parents, relatives, and friends saved to give to me upon my return. The letters I selected begin with my arrival in Vietnam and chronicle my odyssey to Cambodia. Read chronologically, they comprise a coherent recount of those events, a story. Specifically, I want to address the last letter. After just over a week on the Cambodian border, my platoon entered Cambodia for a week. During that week Cambodia was bucolic. After, we returned to Vietnam for a week to perform maintenance on our tracks (armored personnel carriers) and trucks. Finally, we reentered Cambodia for just over three weeks before returning to Vietnam. Most of the fighting my platoon engaged in occurred during those last weeks. That's the period during which my "The Reluctant Tunnel Rat" vignette experience occurred.

Finally, for some, the title of this book, *God Said Let There Be Light And There Was "LLUMO,"* may deserve some explanation. Perhaps you have asked what is LLUMO? LLUMO is military slang for illumination. Specifically, it refers to parachute flares. Such flares are used to illuminate the battlefield at night. Flares may be deployed by artillery, mortars, dropped from a helicopter, or by an individual soldier using a handheld launcher or an M79 grenade launcher. If needed and with the right support, flares may be maintained over an engaged unit for extended periods of time. And there is a genesis for the title. You will meet Indian Jo in chapter 4, "Letters Home from the Front." I don't know whether it was an original Indian Jo comment, or he heard it somewhere, but when the flares were up he would often say: "God said let there be light and there was LLUMO." Also, as sort of a temporary tattoo from the war, I fired so many hand-launched flares that I had a half circle of deeply embedded powder burns, from the launch rocket back blast, at the base of my left thumb, for years after I left Vietnam. As the burns faded they were like a transient brand and a constant reminder of a hard reality slowly dissolving into memory.

Introduction

IF THE READER has a smartphone or tablet, then he/she has probably filled out some form online whereby the reader had to enter his/her birthdate. Usually there are three windows: one for month, one for day, and one for year. When touching the screen, they roll through the numbers like a spinning slot-machine reel. When you spin through the twelve months and the thirty-one or less days, no problem. But spinning through the years can induce contemplation, depending upon one's age. I turned seventy-one in December 2017, so every time I spin the year reel back to 1946, spinning thorough the decades causes me to reflect. This book is essentially the product of reflection and contemplation. Much of what I've written are my attempts to recapture earlier times, good and bad, in my life. But these are just glimpses.

As I wrote the vignettes that comprise this book, my mind kept conjuring memories of many events concurrent with the timeframe and place covered by the vignette. Some of my friends who have read these vignettes were triggered to identify with the place, time, or event described, which opened pathways through our joint memories, leading to reminiscent discussions. Perhaps the reader, regardless of age or where he/she grew up, will relate to my presentation of the events described. If so, maybe pathways in the reader's memory will be stimulated, allowing the reader, pleasurably I hope, to follow his/her own reflections. I am confident that this will occur in the case of readers that, to some extent, were physically, emotionally, or both, connected to some of the national events described.

Before the reader launches into the rest of this book, let me remind you that, in the Preface above, my Vietnam experience caused me to ask two questions: "Where am I?" and "Where was I?" Those questions can be extrapolated to the soul-searching questions we have all asked ourselves: "What's my life all about?" and "What does it mean?" My return visit to Vietnam, during 2016, allowed me to partially answer my original questions. After my return to Vietnam, I cruised up the Mekong River and crossed from Vietnam into Cambodia. Upon leaving Vietnam, I wrote the following in my journal: "Imagine that a long time ago you were reading the only copy of the most vivid novel you ever read. And just as you got to the last chapter you lost the book. For the next 46 years you've wondered how the story ended. Then one day you find the book and are able to read that last chapter. And it's the best ending you could possibly have imagined. With a peaceful sense of satisfaction, you close the book and put it back on the shelf." That's the kind of progress we all seek to achieve as we live out our lives. I'm still working on my personal progress. I am confident the reader is as well. We all seek LLUMO.

Chapter 1
The Formative Years

Growing up in Houston

I WAS BORN in 1946 at Houston Baptist Hospital on South Main. I believe now it is Herman Memorial in the Houston Medical Center, one of the largest medical centers on the planet. When I was six, had my tonsils removed, probably at Baptist, ether as anesthetic. I remember screaming loudly as they placed the ether-soaked rag over my face, then nothingness. It was my first Jean Paul Sartre experience: *Being and Nothingness*.

In the mid-forties, there were about 500,000 folks living in Houston. There are almost 2,500,00 in the city limits now. My grandfather, David Raymond Luce, moved to Houston in the late 1800s and was working for a Houston newspaper in 1900. He and my grandmother, Addie, built a house in the Houston Heights in 1911. Believe I qualify as a true native.

My dad, Wilbert, and mom, Norma, built their house in Park Place, a Houston suburb seven miles southeast of downtown. They built in the late thirties. Land and new house cost $3,500. Soon after, Pearl Harbor shook the country. My dad and two of his brothers enlisted in the Navy. Dad told me he saw men with babies saying goodbye to their wives at the Houston train station as they shipped out to the war. He was married to Mom but no children and told me he couldn't bear staying at home waiting for the draft while these other men were volunteering. So, he volunteered.

After the war, I was part of the leading edge of the "baby boomer" generation. What a ride. Grew up in the Park Place Baptist Church on Broadway; Methodist Church was next door. Never understood the difference. Around the corner and a couple of blocks down was Saint Christopher's Catholic Church. Understood the difference there—annual bizarre included gambling and beer. I was too young for either but loved it. Maybe should have been a Catholic? Pope Pius XII died in 1958. First Pope to die in my lifetime. Saint Christopher's door was shrouded in black bunting.

Downtown Houston was 1920s to 1930s skyscrapers. The Esperson buildings were the tallest, one about twenty floors and the other about thirty floors. Watched the skyline grow to today's amazing extent. Remember the first true skyscraper, the Exxon Building: forty-four floors and the tallest building west of the Mississippi when built in 1963. I was seventeen. Great place for a date; had a viewing floor at the top. On a clear night, could see the lights of Houston 360 degrees. Realized I was living in a big, big city.

I remember the first freeway built, the Gulf Freeway. Was completed in 1952. It's still under construction and always will be. I was six or seven but remember climbing a tree in Jerry Long's backyard (house near the freeway) and watching the construction. Now, almost sixty-five years later, Houston has one of the most expansive freeway systems on the planet.

Attended Park Place Elementary, which was catty-corner from Saint Christopher's. Park Place was one of Houston's first suburbs located about seven miles from downtown Houston. Was built in the 1930s. Park Place was a special place in the early fifties: blue-collar, working dads back from the war and moms having babies, us baby boomers. Park Place Elementary was a neighborhood school and most of us walked to school. I did.

I began kindergarten in 1952, in Mrs. Hurlbert's class in the WWII "shacks" behind the old, main building. There was no air conditioning and Houston is in the hot south. The only relief was open windows without screens. First grade was in the original, main building. But after, back to the shacks, and I had to work my way up to the status of classes in the main building. I'm thinking fifth grade I made it back to the main building. Lunch in the cafeteria, located upstairs in the main building, was always there for all.

Wasn't long after WWII and the Cold War was raging. The Houston air-raid sirens wailed every Friday at noon and we had weekly bomb drills in the halls: out of our classes and into the halls, duck and cover! Essentially, babies huddled in front of the hall lockers, preparing for a Soviet nuclear strike. Showed us films, over and over, of the devastation of a nuclear bomb. Plus, we were constantly shown movies about the communist threat to our survival. Maybe that's what screwed up so many people growing up in the fifties and sixties. And still dealing with Russia and North Korea? Where's the gin?

But Park Place Elementary was fabulous. Fall Festival was the best. Our parents turned our little campus into a fun fall bizarre. Dozens of game booths. Food. Music. Fun. Laughter. The delights that make a wonderful childhood. Fabulous! Loved Park Place Elementary. The oak trees. Flag detail: got to wear a special white belt with shoulder harness and raise the American flag every morning. Safety detail: got to wear an even cooler harness and hold a cane fishing pole with a stop sign on the end and block traffic each morning and afternoon so classmates could safely cross the street. Stopping a car. First sense of empowerment. Responsibility. Growing up.

Park Place Polio Pioneers

THE MOST RIVETING experience of my young life at Park Place Elementary was the plague of polio.

My classmates, and churchmates, were being decimated. Braces, wheelchairs, iron lungs. Wasted lives. Earlier, FDR was crippled from polio, but this epidemic was different. It was pervasive. All were touched. All were in fear. My mom hung a phosphoresce Jesus on the wall in my bedroom, not because of the polio plague, just because she was a devout Christian. The Jesus glowed at night. Some nights I asked him to spare me from polio—and, if my younger brother Kenneth peed in the bed, to protect me from the wet spot.

In defense of a defenseless generation, Jonas Salk produced a polio vaccine. But it had to be tested. In 1954, at Park Place Elementary, in the second-floor cafeteria of the main building, me and my classmates, seven- or eight-year-old test subjects, lined up for shots ("Polio Pioneers"—I believe I still have my card). No one knew whether they were getting the trial vaccine, which had the potential to induce polio, or a placebo. All us kids were crying because we hated shots. I was terrified. Parents freaking out. A needle broke off in Ronnie Bopp's arm. Crying intensified. Parents putting their children on the line. That was Park Place Elementary at its

6

finest. And we defeated polio—one of the greatest achievements during my lifetime. Rivals the lunar landing. Salk never sought a patent for his vaccine. Once, a famous reporter, Edward R. Morrow, asked him why? Salk replied, "How do you patent the Sun?" What a fabulous human being.

Papa

PAPA, JOHN HOWARD King, was my mother's stepfather. Her father, my biological grandfather, Ellis Lee Brooks, died when I was about five—just a vague memory. To me, Papa was my grandfather. He worked as a driller in the oilfields all his life. Drilled wells in Texas, Louisiana, and Oklahoma. There was a drilling crew. They all had nicknames. Papa, the driller (the guy in charge), was "King," of course. But there was "Slim," "Mudge," and many others that I can't recall. The drilling crew operated like gypsies.

The crew was self-contained: trucks to carry the drilling rig (the "tower"), boilers, drill pipe, planks to build roads through the mud to the rig, and tons of other stuff it took to set up a well. There were key terms like "setting-up tower" and "tearing down tower," which meant the crew just arrived at a new location or were preparing to move to a new location. When setting-up tower, space had to be cleared and board roads had to be installed to the drill site. Rattlesnakes were everywhere. Traditionally, the snakes that had to be killed were hung on a fence. It was around these hard working "roughnecks," as they were called, that I grew up—salt of the earth folks.

Beginning when I was about nine and continuing until I was twelve or thirteen, during every summer break from school my parents shipped me off to spend two or three weeks with my grandparents, Grandma Mildred and Papa. Each summer was in a different small town in Texas or Louisiana. As mentioned above, the drilling crew moved around. Grandma and Papa would rent a small apartment, or a trailer house, in town and Papa would drive to the rig every day. Often Grandma and I would go with him and spend the day around the rig. Usually there were ponds near the rig and Grandma and I fished. What we caught would be dinner that evening back in town. Sometimes there was a creek near the rig and Grandma would take me swimming. Sometimes we just hung out around the rig.

Grandma and Papa had a single-shot .22-caliber rifle that only fired 22 shorts. By the time I was eleven or twelve they let me run around with the .22 in the woods near the rig and hunt for squirrels and rabbits. Don't remember bagging any, but if I had, I'm pretty sure that would have been on the menu that evening back in town. Also, by that time Grandma and Papa were pretty much letting me run around the drill site unsupervised. I'm not sure they appreciated that an eleven- or twelve-year-old kid feels pretty bullet proof.

The rigs in those days were steam driven. Big boilers produced the steam and live-steam pipes moved the steam to the drilling platform to turn the drill pipe. The drill was attached to the pipe and did it's work at the bottom of the hole. Mud, called drilling fluid, was pumped down the hole and it created enough friction to prevent the pipe from blowing out of the hole, if gas pressure built up at the bottom of the well. Spent mud was pumped into a slush pit near the rig. The pit was dug while setting-up tower. The mud remained viscous in the slush pit but a thin layer on top hardened and looked like solid ground, unfortunately for me.

One day I was just fooling around the drill site; I believe I was shooting at tin cans with the .22. In any case, something caught my attention a good distance away, maybe a rabbit. So, I ran toward whatever it was. Distracted, I ran right into the slush pit and immediately broke through the thin, dry crust. I began to sink into the mud, but just above me was a pipe. I grabbed it to pull myself out, but it was a live-steam pipe, which is extremely hot. The skin on my left hand and forearm were well seared and I screamed for help. One of the roughnecks was nearby and pulled me out. Of course, there was a trip to the doctor in town. I was OK, only ointment and bandages for a few weeks, but I believe Grandma and Papa were very worried.

After those years around the rigs, I hung out with Papa a lot. We tended his large garden together. We fished. When I began duck hunting in high school, I brought my ducks to Papa and he would clean them for me. I always begged him to go hunting with me, but he never did. However, just before I left for Vietnam, he told me that when I returned we would hunt some ducks together.

As a tribute, during WWII, Papa drilled wells. The nation needed oil. Grandma worked at a shipyard as a welding cutter, cut out patterns from steel plates for use to build ships. I hope the pictures of Papa below portray to the reader the power of these uncomplicated people that did so much to secure for us the wonderful lives we enjoy today.

Papa working on the drilling platform.

*Papa (standing right) and a roughneck
handling drill pipe on the turntable.*

Pine Gully and a Hidden Pack of Parliaments

SEVEN MILES SOUTH of downtown Houston there was a special neighborhood named Park Place. Just prior to WWII, Mom and Dad built a house there. My younger brother, Kenneth, and I grew up there, along with all my Park Place Elementary friends. It was a great time, mid-fifties and early sixties.

We all played outdoors all the time and roamed far from home. Don't remember any safety worries. When it was time to come home, I could hear my mom's "call home" from at least a block away. Phil Hubbard's mom rang a cowbell, which could be heard up to two blocks away. Dozens of families and triple the dozens of kids grew up in Park Place.

We all walked to Park Place Elementary, which was three blocks from my house on Hartford. By ten or eleven we were all equipped with bikes. Liberating! Parents probably never had a clue where or how far we rode. If they knew, would have probably had a cardiac. But wasn't just about bikes. They just got us to the action. One of the greatest attractions was Pine Gully.

The Gully Bridge, a pedestrian bridge over Pine Gully, was special. City-maintained, made of wood. It was the only way to cross Pine Gully from Broadway to Old Galveston Highway, Highway 3. Could be two of us or could be six-plus, more or less—just short of *Lord of the Flies*, running wild along the banks of Pine Gully, sometimes with BB Guns, sometimes fishing for crawfish. A creek ran through Pine Gully. Always exploring. We were essentially feral children. Then one day, the mother lode. We were maybe thirteen or fourteen.

Under the Gully Bridge, probably hidden by another *Lord of the Flies* band, was a pack of Parliament cigarettes and a book of matches. Big moral decision. None of us had ever smoked. All had been schooled in either the Baptist or Methodist church. Mortal sin. Soul cast into hell. Plus, if Mom and Dad found out, instant death. But most of our dads smoked. Do we light up? After brief discussion we, of course, did. Got dizzy. Think John David puked. But had my first cigarette. Don't worry. Never a smoker.

Growing up with a Friend

I HAD A longtime friend, Tom Hannsz. Tom's dad, Elmer, and my dad, Wilbert, attended Rice Institute together during the Great Depression. It always pleased me that there was an intergenerational aspect to our friendship. I met Tom at Park Place Baptist Church and we often sat together during the Sunday service. We attended Park Place Elementary together, but Tom was a half grade ahead of me, so we didn't share any classes. But we were on our way to many adventures together.

We were both in Boy Scout Troop 17 and, beginning around age twelve, spent many years camping together with the Troop. It was little more than twelve years after the end of WWII and our leaders, most combat veterans, perceived us as small soldiers in boot camp. Tom and I always loved the military feel and we worked hard to make rank. Tom made Eagle before me, but I caught up and we remained in the Troop together until the end of high school. Our Eagle training served us well in years to come.

Tom's dad owned Diamond Supply, a mill supply company on Harrisburg toward downtown Houston from Park Place. I began working there with Tom when I was fourteen: Saturdays during school and full time during summer vacation. Even when I went on to other endeavors, I worked there with Tom on Saturdays until I graduated from college—eight years in all. Tom and I loved it: working in the warehouse with the warehousemen, manually punching holes in probably five hundred miles of conveyor belt so the millwrights at the local rice mills and coffee plants could bolt material handling buckets to the belt and finally, when we were old enough to get our commercial drivers licenses, delivering supplies to the rice mills and coffee plants, and other factories, along the Houston ship channel. Along with church and Scouts, Diamond Supply was a tremendously formative experience for both of us.

For years, beginning in high school and through college, Tom and I hunted ducks every season with his uncle, Corky. We went on three or four hunts a year. Corky always put Tom and me together in a blind. Hunt days we were heading out of Park Place by 4:00 a.m., on our way to Old and Lost River in upper Trinity Bay. After a couple of long, cold boat rides up bayous and a hike through swamp, we had our decoys out and were in the blind just as the sun came up. You learn a lot about someone after sharing a shivering duck blind for innumerable hours over many years. I learned a lot about Tom— not least, he was a good shot.

Tom and I attended Milby High School. During high school, Tom got his first car, a green 1957 Ford Fairlane. On weekends, we used to cruise the Princess Drive-In, up-and-down South Main, the ICEE (where Reveille and Telephone intersect) and the Chuck Wagon on Broadway (last on the list but not unproductive), a couple of 16-year-old guys thinking about girls 110 percent of the time. No low-t issues then. No cool. No girls. So, Tom loved to shop for sunglasses (Lang's or Harris's drug store, maybe Foley's) and cologne (Canoe was his favorite). He even glued some fifty-nine Caddie taillights over the taillights of the Fairlane. Tom moved on to pipes in college. I believe it was a Hugh Heffner thing. He also moved up to a 1962 Pontiac Grand Prix. That definitely improved our odds.

My dad had a fishing/ski boat that I commandeered when I was sixteen. Beginning then and through most of college, Tom, David Lott, J.W. Hansen, Don Thompson, and I spent endless summers skiing the San Jacinto River and Taylor Lake. In a day we would burn through twenty-two gallons of gas and sometimes go buy more. Importantly, taking girls skiing was a good way to impress them. But there was an issue. These were the days of surfing and the Beach Boys. Water skiing wasn't "in." So, Tom and I made protest signs, taped them to our skis and picketed KILT radio station because they were playing too much surfing music.

President John F. Kennedy (JFK) visited Houston the day before he was assassinated in Dallas. As planned, he landed at Hobby Airport and his motorcade moved down Broadway to the Gulf Freeway on the way to the Rice Hotel. Tom and I parked his car right on the Broadway curb and were standing on the hood when JFK came by. We were less than ten feet from his open limousine as it passed and, moving slowly, he looked us both in the eyes for a couple of brief seconds.

Tom joined Milby's Reserve Officers Training Corps (ROTC) and convinced me to do the same. We enjoyed it and I, in particular, learned a lot that would benefit me later. Tom remained in ROTC through college; I didn't. At the end of college, when it was time for Tom to enter the Army as an officer, he served two years as an MP, but they discovered he had a heart issue and he was medically disqualified from service. I wasn't disqualified; I was drafted into the Army immediately after graduation from the University of Houston and ended up in a mechanized infantry unit in Vietnam. That was a pretty tough gig after growing up in the comfort of Park Place. But I had several lifelines back home; besides my mom, Tom was one of them. He sent me care packages from home: some food treats unavailable to us there, books, magazines, and anything else I wrote and asked him for. I believe, in a vicarious way, because we were so close, he was fulfilling a dream, at least in part, through me.

Tom's brother, Don, was graduating from Annapolis about the time Tom and I graduated from Milby. Don was home during the summer of 1964, during which time their father died from a massive heart attack. Don was driving back to Annapolis with another Midshipman, Tommy Newell. Tom and I rode with them. We passed through DC the day President Johnson signed the 1964 civil rights bill, and spent a week with Don and his girlfriend's family at a vacation community on the Severn River near Annapolis. We had a great time water skiing on the Severn. Also, Don's future brother in law loaned us his Austin Healy for the week. The northern girls dug our southern accents—much accentuated once we figured that out. The down side was that Tom and I had to ride a Greyhound bus back to Houston: forty-four hours. But there were a couple of girls on the bus on their way home to Rosenberg, a small town south of Houston, so we made the best of it.

During college at the University of Houston, Tom and I pledged Pi Kappa Alpha (ΠKA) fraternity. We had some good times, but Tom didn't like the hazing and dropped out. So, Tom was the ROTC and I was the Greek. But he came to some of our ΠKA parties after that. Lots of fun. Think *Animal House*.

About the second year at U of H, we rented an apartment

together in the Houston Montrose. It was the first time either of us lived away from our parents. What fun! Eventually the finances weren't there and we both moved back home.

The summer of 1965 I convinced Tom to go to Mexico. We flew to Mexico City and spent a few days there. We actually did some cultural activities: National Anthropological Museum in Chapultepec Park, Ballet Folkloric in the National Art Palace and the pyramids at Teotihuacán. Then we flew to Acapulco. Splendid. Amazing. Beyond all expectations. The Rolling Stones had just released "Satisfaction" and we immediately met five guys our age from England. The leader's name was Dave. Hell, they may well have been the Dave Clark Five. The seven of us, and various hangers-on, spent the next five days (mostly nights) in the go-go clubs: Whisky Au Go-Go, Tequila Au Go-Go, and Aka Tiki. Fabulous! We went back to Acapulco the next summer but skipped Mexico City. Another great trip, but without the Brits. However, we did learn to SCUBA in the Pacific. When Tom got home he bought a set of gear, but I don't believe he thought that through. Not many SCUBA opportunities around Houston. But we did put the gear to use scouring the bottoms of the ponds in Glenbrook Golf Course for balls at 2:00 a.m. in the morning, which we sold back to the golfers at the clubhouse the next day. Good source of extra income.

Tom and I always liked the thought of flying. We used to go to the private plane showrooms around Hobby Airport just to look and dream. About the second year at the U of H we entered ground school at Hull Field in Sugar Land, which we completed and passed the test. Then we were assigned to our planes and instructors. After about seven or eight hours we both soloed. It took forty-five flying hours to get a private pilot license—a substantial amount with an instructor, but the majority practicing solo. We solo practiced together and tore up the skies around Houston. One day we were practicing touch-and-go landings at various airports: La Porte, Spaceland, and Scholes Field at Galveston, all uncontrolled. Tom was a good pilot and flew by the book. Me, not so much. Maybe a little Pete Mitchell there. We were approaching Spaceland Airport and the pattern was empty. Tom lined up to make a normal approach and enter the downwind leg. I realized I was in position to enter immediately on base and radioed Tom to tell him that's what I was going to do. In freeway-driving terms, it would be like recklessly cutting someone off to beat them to an exit ramp. So, I landed ahead of him, taxied to the office, parked, went in and got a Coke. When Tom got down and was in the office, he was pissed. Rightly. This wasn't the Gulf Freeway in your lane at 60 mph. It was a couple of planes flying at more than double that and no brakes. The only way Tom could have been angrier was if he found me sniffing around a couple of his girlfriends. Anyway, I hung my head in feigned shame and, after he let me suffer a minute or so, he forgave me. All back to normal.

Beginning the second year of college, I went to work for NASA in the Public Affairs Office at the Manned Spacecraft Center (MSC) by Clear Lake. Later, my boss asked me if I would take over responsibility for the Sunday public open house, which I did. But I needed someone to help me and, at my request, he hired Tom. So, for a couple of years Tom and I spent our Sundays hosting thousands of visitors to MSC: introducing NASA films in the auditorium, answering questions and explaining exhibits in the museum. Like everyone else, astronauts have friends and family that visit them on Sundays and they would bring them to the center. Several knew Tom and would ask him for help briefing their visitors. For example,

Denton Cooley, the renowned Houston heart surgeon, came down with Christian Barnard, the South African heart surgeon who performed the first heart transplant, and a busload of Houston high rollers. Jim Lovell (Gemini 7 and 12 and Apollo 8 and 13), working with Tom and I, was the official host. Tom had the opportunity to spend personal time with Astronaut Lovell, among others. For young guys like us, professional experiences like that put us mentally way ahead of the game.

After Vietnam, I came back to Houston and worked Apollo flight 15, then went to work for Braniff International airlines in New Orleans. I was there the next fourteen years. During those years, Tom graduated from law school and built a successful practice. After I returned to Houston, at age forty, I entered law school. After graduation and admittance to the State Bar, I went to work for Tom. He was an astute lawyer. I learned a lot from him about the law and its practice. Unfortunately, Tom passed away at age forty-six (July 28, 1946 to January 24, 1992).

Martin Luther King, Cassie, and Me

FIRST, I MUST lay the predicate. I grew up in the late forties through the late sixties in Park Place, a Houston suburb, seven miles southeast of downtown Houston. My mom and dad built a house there in the late thirties.

As far back as I can remember, we had two black maids, Clarise and Cassie. Clarise worked all day Monday through Friday. Cassie came once a week to iron. Those ladies helped raise me from the time I was a baby until I graduated from college. My mom and dad bonded with them, as did I. Initially, Clarise rode the bus to the corner a half block down from my house to come to work. In later years, she arrived in her Cadillac. By then, I believe, working for my mom and dad was more than that. It was a friendship that was difficult to have in the south in those days and the work routine was just a way to cover for the underlying mutual love and respect. Clarise's husband, Grissom, and my dad became good friends. A vignette from that relationship follows.

Dad's friendship with Grissom was not casual. They were still friends when my dad was in his late seventies and early eighties, before he had to go to assisted living. During those years, Dad's doc told him to drink a couple of cans of Ensure every day to "ensure" he was getting enough nutrients. Great, except Ensure was very expensive. As it turns out, Dad was complaining to Grissom (same age as Dad) about the price and Grissom had a solution. Grissom had some kind of black market connection to acquire Ensure on the cheap and he offered to let Dad get in the clandestine circle. Dad agreed. I remember the deliveries. Grissom would pull into the driveway and open the trunk. He and Dad would look around like an FBI agent was behind every tree. Then they would surreptitiously transport several cases of Ensure to Dad's garage. High crimes and misdemeanors!

The year of 1968 was tough for our country. I remember the day Martin Luther King Jr. was assassinated, April 4, 1968. There was unrest in the black communities. That night I was driving north on Highway 59/45 just southeast of downtown Houston. Off to the left, around Texas Southern University, I could see fires burning in the black neighborhoods. It was a terrible day in our history. Five days later, April 9, was his nationally televised funeral. I watched his funeral with Cassie on Dad's old color TV.

I will never forget. It was just me and Cassie. I was in Dad's chair in front of the TV. Cassie was just behind me dipping snuff and ironing. The "pomp and ceremony" of Martin Luther King Jr.'s funeral was playing out on the TV. I don't remember whether there were old negro spiritual songs on TV and Cassie sang along or Cassie was just singing a cappella behind me. But I listened to her sing and reflected with her. And, with Cassie, I mourned the loss of an important American.

CHAPTER 2
THE SPACE PROGRAM

NASA and the Manned Spacecraft Center

BEFORE I DETAIL some of my experiences at The National Aeronautics and Space Administration (NASA) and the Manned Spacecraft Center (MSC), I must lay the predicate. During the late sixties, there were several of us protocol officers working in the Public Affairs Office (PAO) handling all level of MSC visitors, including super-level VIPs. We got our assignments on blue NASA forms, like a work order. It gave us the group name and number, or the individual's name, and a description of the tour/escort-services to be provided. The level of importance of the visitor could be divined from the requirements. If the order stated technical briefers all locations, astronaut briefing at the Mission Control Center (MCC), and photographer, then you knew you were dealing with somebody with stroke. But a lot of the folks I showed around were just interesting people that somehow got a private tour of MSC.

I wore a red security badge, meaning I had a secret security clearance. Essentially, I could go anywhere on the center unchallenged. And, after a year or so, all the security guards knew me so well that I believe I could have walked into MCC, during a mission, without a badge and without challenge. The other cool aspect of my job was setting up the tours. For the VIPs, and some were technical (e.g., engineers or scientists), I had to schedule the appropriate sites to visit (e.g., training facilities, centrifuge, space suit lab, laser test range, vacuum chambers, anechoic chamber, etc.) and arrange for technical briefers. If an astronaut was included, I had to schedule that with the astronauts' office and arrange for a photographer. We had two fulltime NASA photographers that I worked with for all those years. The top of the food chain was an astronaut briefing at MCC with photographs. I worked with all the astronauts: Mercury, Gemini, and Apollo, but mostly Gemini and Apollo. They had what they called the day "in the barrel," meaning they rotated days to fit in meeting and briefing visitors with their training schedules. If an astronaut was in the barrel, he had the duty. This was all fascinating and I was essentially an intelligent parrot. After hearing hundreds of technical briefings from rocket scientists, engineers and astronauts at all the facilities at MSC and being semi-intelligent, plus a sponge, I really learned a lot about what was going on there— eventually enough to brief technical groups at most facilities without assistance.

Ray W. Luce (left) with visitor at MSC.

Test Subject

I JOINED NASA early in 1966 as a test subject. I participated in a stress test whereby NASA was studying a person's ability to concentrate on a task while under extreme stress. Following instructions, I drove from Houston down to the Manned Spacecraft Center (MSC) near Clear Lake. I checked in at the security office near the main entrance and spoke with one of the security officers. He called my contact, a psychologist or psychiatrist (not sure which), and in a few minutes the doctor, white coat and all, arrived in a NASA station wagon and drove me to the astronauts' office building.

After spending a couple of hours in a lab room with the docs in the white coats and having electrodes attached to various parts of my body, they drove me to a small lab at the back of the MSC site. I was seated in a Mercury capsule mock-up and the electrodes were attached to various apparatus. My task was to monitor a control panel and, with certain buttons and switches, keep all the dials centered. The docs told me I would hear bells periodically and, when the bells stopped, I would receive a small electric shock through my left calf. Just before they shut the hatch to the capsule, one of the docs pointed to a switch. He said, "This is the 'chicken switch.' If you can't proceed with the test, throw the switch and we'll let you out." He probably knew that the odds of a young guy from Texas pulling that switch, once the concept of "chicken" was introduced, were slim to none. Then they shut the hatch and it was pitch black, except for the dials I had to monitor and manipulate. When the first bells sounded, it was deafening; like a freight train coming through the capsule. When the sound stopped, I instantly received the "small" shock. It was intense and snapped my body rigid. At that point, I knew I was in for a long ride. The freight train came through the station thirteen times followed by twelve shocks. When the thirteenth train came through there was no shock and the hatch opened. I had been in the capsule almost three hours. The docs showed me some of the strip charts recording my biometrics: off the chart with the first bells and shock, and almost the same for the last bells and the hatch opening.

It wasn't a fun experience, but I was proud to have somehow contributed, even in such a relatively small way, to the goal JFK set for us in 1961 to land Americans on the moon and return them safely to Earth by the end of the decade.

The Rifleman

TO PARAPHRASE SECRETARY of Defense Donald Rumsfeld, "There are known knowns, known unknowns, and unknown unknowns; the latter are the most difficult to deal with." NASA's prime directive was to protect the life and safety of the astronauts. Part of that were the practices of modularization and redundancy. All systems had double, triple, and more redundancy. But even so, it was difficult to plan for those "unknown unknowns."

I received the blue form a few days ahead. Fun assignment: approximately three hundred Cub Scouts and their leaders, NASA film in the auditorium, and a museum visit. Easy enough. Plus, I was a Cub Scout, Boy Scout, and made Eagle Scout. I liked the Scout movement. I was looking forward to this group. I knew the energy level of a few busloads of Cubs. I was ready.

The call came in from the main security gate. The Cubs were here, and the buses were headed for the museum. I went outside to meet them. Six or eight standard-issue, yellow school buses pulled up and began to unload. As it turned out, all the Cubs were from black Cub Packs. Not uncommon segregation in Houston during the sixties. As they unloaded, the fun began. Three hundred eight-to-ten-year-old Cub scouts in their blue

31

uniforms, blue caps, and yellow scarfs. Enough energy to power a medium-sized city. Shouts, squeals, and laughter sufficient to bring a smile to the face of the most diehard curmudgeon. Their leaders had their hands full. But I knew the drill. That's when the "unknown unknown" presented itself.

I did not know that another protocol officer was finishing a VIP private tour of the Manned Spacecraft Center's facilities with a museum visit. His VIP was Chuck Connors. I was talking with a couple of the Scout leaders to coordinate moving the Cubs into our eight-hundred-seat auditorium in the museum for the film. The other leaders were attempting to keep three hundred smiling, laughing Cubs corralled. Just then, the other protocol officer and Chuck Connors exited the museum near the buses. I had not noticed, but one of the Cubs near me did. My first clue was I heard the Cub scream: "the Rifleman, the Rifleman!" The original series had ended maybe three or four years prior in '63 but was still in constant rerun. *The Rifleman* was a huge hit. And it began.

Like an out-of-control sea in a gale, a wave of three hundred Cubs headed for Chuck Connors—three hundred smiling, shouting, waving, ecstatic Cub Scouts. There was no time to react. In less than a minute, Chuck Connors was surrounded, and I saw this beautiful smile come across his face. This could have been a protocol disaster but in that instant, I knew it was going to be OK.

There he stood, the 6' 5" Rifleman, grinning, smiling, laughing, and waving, surrounded by a laughing, shouting, waist-high, waving sea of black and blue. It was beautiful. I could see a positive energy feedback loop building up. In nuclear parlance, approaching critical mass. Finally, Chuck's protocol officer moved in and extracted him. But what fun. Definitely made me a Chuck Connors fan in the great-human-being category.

Pop Top Technology

I GOT THE blue form a couple of days ahead. Simple assignment: take a South African dentist on the standard private tour. I liked those assignments because, with just one or two visitors, I could take them to really cool background areas that a normal group would never see. I liked those areas myself.

The South African dentist cleared main-gate security and arrived at the museum, our protocol headquarters. I could tell he was a good guy. It was a nice day and we walked to the buildings I had selected for the tour: mission simulators, centrifuge, Mission Control Center, and I threw in a backroom training facility, the neutral bouncy tank.

One of the major challenges of space flight is zero gravity. On earth, there are only two ways to simulate weightlessness: (1) In a KC135 tanker aircraft converted so that the interior is a large, padded room and flying continuous parabolic curves. This will provide twenty to twenty-five seconds of true weightlessness—good training to maybe understand how to move around in a spacecraft while weightless but not enough time for any meaningful training. (2) In a neutral bouncy tank.

The neutral bouncy tank was in a large room in one of the astronaut training buildings. It was about thirty feet in diameter and twenty-plus feet deep. The water was crystal clear. All around, at eye level, there were portholes to view the activity in the chamber. The point of the training was to give the astronauts a near-actual experience of conducting an extravehicular activity (EVA) here on earth. The first astronaut (any human) to perform an EVA was Ed White on Gemini 4 in 1965. He died on the pad in the 1967 Apollo fire, along with Gus Grissom and Roger Chaffe. Very sad. I was at the Manned Spacecraft Center at the time.

This day, there was a workstation simulating a station the astronaut would have to attend during his actual EVA later in Gemini. The way it worked was the astronaut, in his spacesuit (they each had half a dozen custom made), was lowered into the tank. There were a couple of scuba divers in the tank. They skillfully began to attach small lead weights to the astronaut's suit (head, arms, and legs) until he was neutrally buoyant: didn't sink, didn't float, touched lightly, and would continue to spin. Once neutral buoyancy was achieved, they could put the astronaut thorough his training session. Fascinating.

So, the South African Dentist and I spent ten to fifteen minutes viewing through the portholes, watching this process unfold. Finally, I decided it was time to take him to the next stop. He was ready to go as well, and just as we were leaving, I spotted the Coke machine. I asked him if he would like a Coke and he said yes. So, I walked to the machine, put in a quarter (yes twenty-five cents in those days) and the Coke can popped out. I handed it to him. He looked at it and kept looking around like he was lost. I could tell he was confused and I asked him what was wrong. He looked me in the eye and asked me where the opener was. I smiled, took the can out of his hand, and snapped off the pop-top. His face was like the brightest, blinking neon sign you ever saw. I read his mind in an instant. He was from South Africa and had never seen a pop-top. He was absolutely amazed. He was thinking, these Americans are brilliant. I was thinking, this guy just spent fifteen minutes, behind the scenes, watching an American astronaut in a neutral bouncy tank training for a Gemini mission and he is more impressed with our pop-top technology—irony to the tenth power.

Lyndon and the Duke

LYNDON JOHNSON RAN against Barry Goldwater as an opponent to the Vietnam War. But he prosecuted the war anyway and, during 1968, the war was going badly. Protests were so virulent that Johnson couldn't speak in open public assembly. He was limited to government-controlled areas: the decks of aircraft carriers or military bases for example. Needing a venue to speak, the Manned Spacecraft Center (MSC) near Houston was perfect: 1,600 fenced and secured acres. And I was an MSC Protocol Officer. Our group was responsible for all MSC visitors, including presidents, with a lot of help in that case, of course. Johnson was scheduled to visit MSC and deliver a major address.

Two weeks prior to Johnson's visit, the Secret Service arrived and we were assigned to assist them in surveying the areas President Johnson would visit. A tour of the facilities was planned for Johnson, including the mission simulators, centrifuge, vacuum chambers, and mission control. We walked with the Secret Service agents down every hall the president would walk. Any door to a hall without a lock would have a lock installed. All very thorough—understandably. Johnson was in a limousine behind Kennedy in Dallas.

The weather was perfect the day Johnson visited. The base

was secured. Only invited guests, the press, and badged employees were permitted. Outside the museum, where we displayed Mercury, Gemini, and Apollo capsules and other cool space-travel artifacts, maybe two hundred folding chairs, in open air, were set up for guests to hear Johnson's speech—the speech where he would brand the politicians that wanted to cut funding to NASA as "little men with poison pens." The podium he would speak from bristled with microphones. All the networks were there. Nothing new. We were used to working with them during missions.

This is where the Duke comes in. The Duke of Rutland is something like third in line for the Crown. Goes back to the 1300s. It's a British thing. Anyway, this Duke had some stroke and, regardless of Johnson's visit, was granted a private tour of MSC. I was assigned to handle him, his wife, and their twelve-year-old daughter. I met them at the main gate and took the front passenger seat in their limousine. I took them on the standard tour, which was similar to the tour we planned for Johnson later in the day. At the end of the tour, I took them to the museum where Johnson would speak later. When we pulled into the VIP parking space outside the museum and got out of the limo, the Duke noticed the podium with the microphones and the two hundred folding chairs. He straightened his back, looked at me, and said, "What time do I speak?" Hey. I'm just a Houston, Milby High School, nearly redneck. But I know arrogance when I see it. How do you tell the Duke of Rutland that the podium isn't really for him? I finally said something like, "Sir, the president of the United States will be here and speaking later. This is for him." Not to totally destroy the Duke's sense of status, I told him he was welcome to remain for Johnson's speech. He was interested but asked whether he could be seated in the front row.

I informed him that all the seats were reserved, and he would have to stand. He informed me that he and the Duchess were only "permitted" to stand twenty minutes. I told him that was not probable, so he, the Duchess, and the daughter took a hike off the center. Wow! The height of arrogance. But the day wasn't over.

Johnson arrived at the center but not at the museum. His motorcade went directly to the tour of facilities that had been planned. His last stop would be the museum. The plan was for Johnson to park in the prime parking space, our center director's space, Dr. Gilruth (Loved him. Google him. Been in his office many times.). It was just a short walk from the parking space to the museum entrance, and we had over a dozen astronauts lined up to shake Johnson's hand as he walked from his limo to the museum. All planned. Picture perfect. NASA Public Affairs (my group) was giddy. Great pics. Great pub. But Murphy's law kicked in: "If anything can go wrong, it will."

President Johnson's limo pulled into Dr. Gilruth's parking place. The astronauts were lined up to greet Johnson. Everybody was excited to see the President of the United States. But Murphy was there. Remember Johnson's dog, a beagle I think, that Johnson got in trouble for because he held him up by the ears? Well he had that dog in his limo. The door to the limo opened. Everybody was on excited edge to see the president step out. But no, the dog jumped out, ran about ten feet to a fire hydrant, lifted his hind leg, and took a presidential dog piss. While the astronauts and the rest of us were watching the dog take care of his business, almost as an afterthought, Johnson got out of his limousine. Now he was pissed—upstaged by a dog pissing on a fire hydrant. He walked to the dog, grabbed it, and essentially threw it at a

Secret Service agent. Then Johnson straightened his back and walked through the receiving line.

Me, my boss, and my boss's boss were just inside the museum doors to welcome the president. As he entered, he shook our hands one by one. I can tell you that Johnson had a big mitt and a strong grip. As he left us and headed to a Gemini capsule for a briefing, I tried to follow, but I instantly had a Secret Service agent in front of me with his hand on my chest. But close enough for a Milby Buffalo.

After the museum tour, Johnson took the podium and spoke. It was surreal. We were on a secure base. Johnson was at an outside podium in front of two hundred folding chairs. Maybe four or five NASA buildings had windows facing that scene. All those buildings had been cleared of occupants, searched, secured, and locked. All the blinds were closed. Armed security, dressed in black with rifles, were standing on top of each building facing the president, like a deathwatch, while the president spoke. Too soon after the Kennedy assassination, I guess. Amazing day.

The Apollo 11 Lunar Landing and the Golden Greek

APOLLO 11 LAUNCHED Wednesday, July 16, 1969. A few days prior, our Manned Spacecraft Center (MSC) Public Affairs Office (PAO) group went to a twenty-four-hours-a-day operation, in shifts. The lunar landing was scheduled for Sunday the twentieth. I received the blue assignment form over the weekend and was assigned as Wernher von Braun's attending protocol officer the day the landing was scheduled. I had been assigned to him previously when he made routine visits to MSC. This was not routine.

At the end of World War II, the US took custody of several Third Reich rocket scientists; others ended up in the custody of the USSR. Kind of a rough split was we got the ones with the most advanced experience and the commies got the "heavy lift" (big rockets) specialists. Von Braun was our guy. Von Braun was a member of the Nazi party and the SS, but his relationship is reported to have been ambivalent. But he did serve the Reich and invented the V2 rocket, which rained death on Britain. In Apollo, that knowledge, experience, and expertise was directed to more positive creation. Von Braun was the Director of NASA's Marshall Spaceflight Center in

Huntsville, Alabama. There, he created and built Apollo's launch vehicle, the Saturn V—the most powerful rocket ever assembled.

Late Sunday morning, I checked out a white US government Ford station wagon and drove to Ellington Field, a US Airforce reserve base just a few miles down Texas Highway 3 from MSC. With a government vehicle and NASA badge, I was able to pull up on the tarmac by NASA's hangar where von Braun would arrive. On time, a Learjet landed and taxied to the hangar. The Lear shut down and the steps were deployed. Von Braun and a guest deplaned. He recognized me from earlier visits. We shook hands and he introduced me to his guest, Cornelius Ryan, the author of *The Longest Day*, the quintessential book recounting D-Day, which was later made into a movie starring John Wayne. Ryan was at Normandy twice on D-Day. He flew over the beaches early during the invasion, flew back to England, and returned to Normandy later in the day by boat. We shook hands. I was twenty-two years old, Apollo 11 was in lunar orbit preparing to land on the moon, and I was going to share this adventure with these historic figures. That day, the eyes of the world were focused on what was about to be attempted and I had a ringside seat. I can't give you a word to describe how I felt; no such word may exist.

I drove von Braun and Ryan back to MSC, parked in a VIP space, and escorted them to the headquarters building for meetings. I left them there and went to my office next door by the museum. Not long after lunch, I met von Braun and Ryan back at the headquarters building and drove them to the Mission Control Center (MCC). The control room is on the third floor and is familiar to anyone who lived through those days. It was central to many TV reports during Gemini and Apollo; the big rear-projection Eidophor screens across the front wall, the flight consoles, and behind it all there is a seventy-four-seat, glassed-in viewing room. There were five or six rows of seats in the viewing room and behind the last row a long bar-height table for standing viewers. As a protocol officer, I had taken hundreds of MSC visitors to this room and briefed them on MCC operations. I had been there for the last five Gemini missions and all the Apollo missions, unmanned and manned. This was different. This was the fulfillment of President Kennedy's challenge to the nation eight years earlier: "Before this decade is out, of landing a man on the Moon and returning him safely to the earth."

The viewing room was filling-up and I seated von Braun and Ryan in their assigned seats in the front row, immediately behind the Flight Director's console, which was manned by Gene Kranz of Apollo 13 fame. I took a place along the long, standing table at the rear. The lunar module had separated from the command and service modules earlier, and it was near the time to begin the descent to the lunar surface. The activity at the consoles was accelerating. In the viewing room we were hearing the capsule communicator's (CAPCOM) channel, which included the transmission from the crew of the lunar module. As the descent proceeded, an animation of what was transpiring was projected on the big screens across the front of the control room. The animation had the lunar module down a few seconds before the actual landing and that momentous radio transmission from the lunar surface, "Houston, Tranquility Base here. The Eagle has landed." The tenseness in the control and viewing rooms, which felt like a one-thousand-pound weight on your chest, erupted into absolute euphoria. The lunar module would spend the next six hours preparing for mans' first walk on the moon. I made my way to von Braun and Ryan and escorted them to the government station wagon.

There were a lot of conversations with a lot of people between the control room and the lobby of MCC, but we finally made it to the car. There was plenty of time until the walk and von Braun asked me whether we could go to Galveston for seafood. I told him of course and we left MSC, heading for the Gulf Freeway. I decided to take him and Ryan to the Golden Greek. It was just over a half-hour ride to the restaurant. In those days, Texas law prevented the sale of liquor by the drink except in private clubs. So, to get around the law, all really good restaurants had a room set aside as a private club, annual membership three dollars. We parked and walked into the Golden Greek.

I knew I had to get von Braun and Ryan into the Golden Greek's private club. It occurred to me that every TV in the world was tuned in to what was happening in Houston and on the moon that day, and I figured that had some cache. I walked up to the maître de and handed him my NASA Protocol Officer business card. I explained that my guests were Wernher von Braun and Cornelius Ryan, that we were just coming from NASA's Mission Control Center, and asked whether they could use the club. Wow! Like offering a ribeye steak to a hungry dog. It was immediately all hands on deck at the restaurant and the maître de began to lead von Braun and Ryan down the hall to the dining room. I was going to do what any good protocol officer would do—wait. Just then, von Braun turned around and asked me whether I was coming. I told him I would wait but he insisted that I join them for dinner. It began to really sink in that I was experiencing something I had never and would never again.

I can't tell you what I ordered, but I remember that there

were crackers and a bowl of horseradish sauce on the table for making cocktail sauce to go with oysters on the half shell. Von Braun opened crackers and smeared them with the horseradish sauce as an appetizer. Must have been hungry, or maybe it's just a German thing. For the next hour or so, I was mesmerized as von Braun and Ryan discussed their helicopter pads and riding miniature submarines around the reefs of Bermuda. Von Braun was ebullient. He was enjoying a great seafood dinner in the Golden Greek's private club while Armstrong and Aldrin were on the lunar surface preparing for their walk on the moon—and his creation got them there.

After dinner, we left the Golden Greek and drove back to MCC for the walk. Heavy stuff!

The Apollo 11 Moon Walk and the Big Pre-Internet "Share"

AFTER DINNER AT the Golden Greek, I drove von Braun and Ryan back to our Manned Space Craft Center (MSC). I escorted them to the control room and seated them again in the front row. The activity on the consoles was intense. The walk was impending and was scheduled to last over two hours. After the walk and Armstrong and Aldrin were back in the lunar module, and the module was sealed, pressurized, and they were safe, my only remaining assignment was to drive von Braun back to the MSC auditorium for the post-walk press conference. Given the two-plus hours, I decided to leave the control room and join my colleagues at the auditorium to view the walk.

The auditorium had eight hundred seats. The entrances were from the front hall of the museum through richly dark, heavy wood doors on each end of the auditorium. The seating area was sunken and sloped down, with three to four continuous steps, back to front the length of the seating, leading up to four spaced doors exiting to the side foyers of the museum, which connected the front hall to the very large rear hall and to many double doors to the outside—first-class. If you are from that era, you would recognize the setting. Post-flight (and some tragic non-flight) press conferences were televised from there. The front and rear halls comprised the museum. In the front hall, there was an actual lunar module that would never fly, one of the Gemini capsules that had flown, space-suit displays, and other cool stuff. In the rear hall there was an Apollo capsule (at that time, probably Apollo 7), a Mercury capsule, and tons more. The museum and auditorium were the heartbeat of our Public Affairs Office (PAO) press operations during missions.

About two weeks prior to a mission, MSC was essentially closed to the public, the museum was cleared of many displays, and those were replaced with rows of long tables in the front and rear halls. Phone lines were run, and phones installed. Electric outlets were installed. All this was in anticipation of the hundreds of press representatives that would invade us for the missions. For Apollo 11, the size of the press corps and the infrastructure needed to support them was on the steroid scale. I don't recall the exact number, but it was close to eight hundred—at least half foreign press from pretty much every country on the globe with an airport.

PAO was divided into two groups, the public information officers who handled the press and the protocol officers who handled all MSC visitors. During missions, protocol officers, like me, were drafted to assist handling the press. As far as knowledge of the NASA/MSC operations, we were probably better informed. If we weren't with a visitor listening to technical briefings from engineers, space scientists, or astronauts, or briefing on our own, we were in our offices studying NASA "fact sheets." These were one-to-many-page technical briefs drafted for technical purposes—not for the public. There was a fact sheet for every aspect of a mission and the hardware involved, from the process of defecating in space to the intricacies of a fuel cell that produced power for the spacecraft. We were knowledgeable.

A few days prior to launch, the press began to arrive. During the next several days, I handled the Argentinian, Israeli, and Japanese contingents, plus others. I escorted these and the others around the center, briefing them on what was going on, including briefings outside Mission Control Center (MCC). There's no doubt I was on national TV (translated) in those countries. Kind of cool to think about—NASA's face broadcast to homes in Buenos Aires. I interacted with many foreign press representatives. They figured out who the public information and protocol officers were and constantly sought us out for information, which I was happy to provide. Sorry for the diversion, but I had to establish the predicate; back to the walk.

I drove from MCC to the museum and found my friends, Tom and Sherry Hannsz. Tom was a protocol officer who helped me run the Sunday MSC public open house. We found seats in the auditorium, which was rapidly filling-up. Eventually, it was standing room only. Humanity was on a threshold. We had a few "all this money for space and no money for the hungry" protesters at the main security gate for a few days. They were peaceful and were invited to join the press in the auditorium. The energy level had been building up for days since launch. Today it kicked into overdrive. It had already been a long day, but no one noticed. Everybody was running on super doses of adrenaline. Probably could have tapped us like maple trees. Energy was reaching a peak. You could feel it, like an electric storm in the Texas hill country moving toward you, lighting and thunder intensifying until reaching a crescendo of flashes and thunder that shakes your bones. Emotionally, that's where those eight hundred-plus of us world citizens in that auditorium were. How do you handle that? And Armstrong's walk began. We watched by way of a black and white projection on a twenty-by-twenty-foot screen at the front of the auditorium. Other than Armstrong's voice, and other than our heartbeats, you could hear a pin drop.

Aldrin and Armstrong were in their pressure suits. The lunar module had been depressurized and the hatch opened. Armstrong began to descend the ladder. There was a final, soft drop to the surface and he spoke those immortal words, "That's one small step for a man; one giant leap for mankind." The Japanese press folks were behind me and didn't quite understand what he said. They were grabbing my shoulder and asking me for translation, which I provided. As Aldrin began to descend the ladder, the entire room was on its feet—some standing on the seats. There was shouting, cheering and jubilation, pandemonium, and this included the international press. Even the protesters joined in the recognition of this fabulous achievement. I knew. Everybody knew. This was the greatest moment in human history. I think we all realized, even if unconsciously, that this moment would never be replicated in our lifetimes. I soaked up that universal energy as long as I could, but I had to return to MCC to bring von Braun back to the auditorium for the post-walk press conference. So, I left.

I entered the control room and found a standing-room spot at the rear table. Witnessing the remainder of the walk in the control room, including Armstrong placing the American flag on the lunar surface, was fascinating. At the end, when Armstrong and Aldrin were back in the lunar module, the module was pressurized, and they were safe. I made my way again to von Braun. Without Ryan, I escorted him to the station wagon and drove him to the auditorium for the post-walk press conference. It was a short drive. I had had dinner with him a few hours earlier and felt like I could describe to him, and he would be interested in, what happened in the auditorium with the press earlier. He was. I described, the foreign and domestic press included, the euphoria, the shouts, standing in the seats, a great human achievement recognized, mankind on the same positive page, and so on. He seemed fascinated. I had just finished my recount as we arrived at the auditorium. We parked, and I escorted him to the long table at the front of the auditorium where the NASA representatives would converse with the world's press. I stood on the side of the auditorium near the conference table. For me, this was heavy, heavy stuff!

The press conference representatives were NASA luminaries: Dr. Gilruth, our MSC director; Dr. Debus, director of the Kennedy Spaceflight Center (also a Nazi and SS member that worked in the V2 program with von Braun); General Phillips, director of the Apollo program and famous for his grave concern for running a 100 percent oxygen environment in the Apollo command module, which unheeded led to the tragic fire; George Mueller, administrator of NASA's manned spaceflight operations; and a couple of others that I don't recall. The press conference began.

Each participant was asked to make a statement, including what the lunar landing and walk meant to mankind. As the answers came, left to right, we heard "like when Columbus discovered America," "like when the wheel was invented," and such. Memory fades but I remember exactly what von Braun said: "Like when our earliest ancestors crawled out of the sea onto the beach." The other guys at the table looked at him and telepathically tried to communicate, "Hey Wernher . . . tone it down." But Wernher wasn't finished. He went on to report that he heard that when Armstrong stepped foot on the moon, in this very auditorium, "foreign and domestic press included, there was euphoria, shouts, standing in the seats, and universal recognition of this tremendous human achievement; a moment when all mankind was on the same positive page." I was stunned. The worldwide TV audience for this seminal event was estimated to be over half a billion—the largest live audience in world history at that time. And this guy just repeated a story I told him less than half an hour earlier. The largest audience, if even second hand, that I will ever have, and the first-ever pre-Internet, thus verbal, "share" to go viral. Humbling.

There is a postscript worth adding. Almost twenty years later, there was a PAO reunion: our leaders, the public information officers, protocol officers, the projectionists up in the auditorium booth, security guards (including a 5′ 5″ great black guy with a heart-melting smile and gold-rimmed teeth that, after Apollo 11, spent every day guarding the moon rocks on display in the auditorium. Nickname: Moon Rock.). Remember that, just after Armstrong and Aldrin set foot on the lunar surface and began the walk, I left the auditorium and returned to the control room. As mentioned, I watched Armstrong plant the American flag on the moon from there. At the reunion I learned from PAO friends that at that moment the foreign press sat down in silence. When the "great achievement for all mankind" became an "American achievement," they lost their enthusiasm.

The Transition

MUST PREFACE THIS. Three events converged during July 1969: I worked Apollo 11 at NASA's Houston Manned Spacecraft Center as a public affairs protocol officer, finished my last course to graduate from the University of Houston, and received my draft notice. It was a confluence of life-changing events. When I received my draft notice, I told my boss that the Apollo 11 splashdown would be my last day at NASA. My plan before induction was to drive my blue 1967 Mustang fastback from Houston to Isla de Mujeres in the Yucatan. Had to have time to reflect and prepare myself mentally for the Army. Saw Isla de Mujeres on a map and decided to head there. Had to report for the draft in just under a month, but after five years in college I wanted to "walk the stage" and receive my degree from the University of Houston, at the end of August, with my mom and dad watching. Wrote my draft board and requested a month's extension to report. Had time for my Yucatan trip regardless but learned extension was approved upon my return to Houston. So, I didn't have to report until September 8, 1969.

I wasn't shocked to receive my draft notice. Expected it as soon as I finished university and lost my student deferment. But it was still disconcerting. I had watched the Vietnam War play out on TV for several years. Watched Walter Cronkite most evenings on CBS. Hundreds of US soldiers were being killed every week during the two years before I was drafted. It wasn't exactly a safe place. I was apprehensive. Needed time to myself to sort out my emotions. I planned my trip to the Yucatan as much as I could. Mustang was in good shape, tires and all. Had an 8-track tape player installed in the dash and plenty of tapes: Jefferson Airplane, Mamas and Papas, Rolling Stones, Beatles, and many more. Had tons of NASA stickers on the back window of the Mustang, including the Apollo 11 mission logo. Since I was working in NASA Public Affairs, I had access to fabulous Apollo 11 photos. I loaded two boxes of 10" by 8" photos into my Mustang. Each box was about five hundred photos. One box was the classic color lithograph of the Apollo 11 crew (Armstrong, Aldrin, and Collins). The other box was a black and white glossy photo of Armstrong on the moon standing in front of the Lunar Module. It was taken right off our Mission Control Center monitors and reproduced to hand out to the press. It had those parallel, horizontal lines that appeared on a photo those days when photographing a TV screen, but it was a clear image of Armstrong and the Lunar Module. So, there I was, a twenty-two-year-old college graduate with a deadline to become a soldier. I had to sort that out. In my Mustang, NASA logos on the windows, and with maybe one thousand classic photos, I left Houston for the Yucatan.

It was a long drive, and all roads were marginal by US standards. First leg was nonstop from Houston to Mexico City. It was just over one thousand miles and took about twenty-seven hours. I arrived in Mexico City early in the day and looked up a girl I had met there in 1966 when traveling there with my buddy, Tom Hannsz. Using a paper map, I located her address and spotted her on the street outside her house. Great reunion. We went to her brother and sister-in-law's apartment in the John F. Kennedy apartment complex. After some food and drink, I crashed there for a lot of needed rest. Great folks to welcome me and give me a place to rest.

Next day, the second leg was Mexico City to Veracruz, about a 263-mile drive through winding mountain roads. On the way I picked-up a hitchhiker between Mexico City and Pueblo. Pueblo is a cool town. The hitchhiker was a young guy about my age. Took him to his house in Pueblo and I took a shower. Then, it was on to Veracruz. I overnighted in a Veracruz hotel. Next leg was Veracruz to Villahermosa, a 290-mile drive. I overnighted in a Villahermosa hotel. Next morning, I took a 90-mile excursion to one of the most famous Mayan ruins, Palenque. Fabulous. Very difficult to get there, and the unpaved road to the site off the two-lane blacktop highway was terrible. Had to be very careful not to bust a tire or break an axle on my Mustang. Made it to the ruins. It was worth the effort—definitely a bucket list item. Palenque is notable because a Mayan king was buried in the main pyramid, Egyptian style. There were rock stairs leading down to his tomb in the center of the pyramid with lights provided by a small gasoline generator. I made it down to the burial chamber. Then, it was on to Campeche, a 327-mile drive from Palenque. Tapes playing, I just kept the wheels turning. I overnighted in Campeche. The final leg was 116 miles to Merida. Between Campeche and Merida, there were roadside food stalls everywhere selling boiled shrimp from the Bay of Campeche with hot sauce. Had a lot. Mistake. Sick a couple of days in a Merida hotel. Drank lots of sparkling mineral water. Decided to skip Isla de Mujeres and headed back to Houston. Retraced my steps, constantly thinking about my impending transition to military life, with the specter of Vietnam in mind.

The trip down to Merida was mostly just about keeping the wheels turning and thinking, but there were some cool experiences on the way south. Once I left Veracruz, I figured out immediately never to pass a Pemex gas station, even if I only needed a couple of gallons (sold by the liter in Mexico) to top off my gas tank. Passed through many, many small villages on the two-lane blacktop highway. Most of the folks were Mayan. Many lived in thatched wooden huts with dirt floors—probably the same for hundreds of years. I passed groups of farmers walking along the highway, all carrying shotguns. It was not drug cartels then; just farmers looking maybe to bag a rogue pig for dinner. Saw some almost stone-age indigent people—they were actually carrying bows and arrows and were very furtive in exposing themselves. In 1969, Yucatan was essentially third world. I pulled into very rudimentary restaurants, or a Pemex, in these small villages. The villagers noticed the Mustang and the NASA stickers and began to check me out. Not much else going on in these small villages. So, they were interested. I would open my trunk and begin handing out the lithographs of the Apollo 11 crew and the glossy photos of Armstrong on the moon. By this time, it had been barely two weeks since the lunar landing and these rural folks knew all about that momentous event. They may have imagined that I was an astronaut. Anyway, at each of these small-village stops, I handed out pictures until the crowds got too large (word spread quickly), and I left for the next stop. I had just completed two years of Spanish at the University of Houston and was able to practice my Spanish with these folks. I got the impression that many spoke Mayan as their first language. It was lots of fun. The pictures I handed out are probably still hanging in their wooden thatched huts. The old timers may remember "the day the astronaut passed through the village." The drive back to Houston was just a "keep the wheels turning" event. It was almost a 4,000-mile roundtrip adventure.

Made it back to Houston and visited Grandma and Papa. Papa had recently retired, and they were heading for Ontario, Canada, for a fishing trip. They had been there the year before and I heard lots of stories about how great it was. Grandma and Papa had a twenty-foot trailer house that they pulled behind Papa's pickup truck. I had heard about their trip the year before. I distinctly remember Papa describing their fishing guide, Indian Joe. Indian Joe was a master fisherman—always put you on the northern pike. After hearing all of Papa's accolades, I pictured Indian Joe as a youthful, invincible, Hiawatha-style Indian. Imagined him as a muscular guy in Indian dress (headband, feather, fringed leather clothes, and gliding across a beautiful Canadian lake in a birchbark canoe). Grandma and Papa invited me to join them and I was immediately onboard. So, we headed for Canada. After a 4,000-mile drive to Yucatan, I was heading to Canada. Papa and I shared the driving and it took four days and three nights to make it to Ear Falls, Canada. We crossed the border at International Falls north of Minneapolis and proceeded to Ear Falls on Lac (lake) Seul. Checked into Lac Seul Lodge on the shore of Lac Seul. It was bucolic. Beautiful. Wonderful. Peaceful. Just what I needed to sort things out with the draft, and I was with the folks I loved the most in my life.

Lac Seul Lodge was wonderful. They had a few spaces for trailer houses, where we parked. Plus, they had a few cabins and a main lodge. We ate most meals in the main lodge. Also, there was a small log-building-type smoker, which was constantly used to smoke meat and fish. There were racks of seasoned meat strips (elk, deer, or moose?) smoking. Plus, there was a hermit that lived on an island nearby who specialized in catching whitefish and preparing them for smoking. The guides, like Indian Joe, always stopped by his island and bought the whitefish for smoking. The freshly smoked meat and fish were off the charts. Also, in the winter, Lac Seul froze several feet deep. Lac Seul Lodge had a low-profile log ice cabin sunk six or so feet into the ground. When the lake was frozen, they took chain saws out on the lake and cut blocks of ice. The blocks were stacked in the ice cabin and insulated with sawdust. The harvested ice would last throughout the summer season. What a great place.

Anyway, I was looking forward to meeting Indian Joe. Once we arrived at Lac Seul Lodge and got settled, Papa and I went to see the owner to plan our fishing. The first thing Papa asked was:

"Where is Indian Joe?"

"He's in the hospital."

"What happened?"

"His brother in law hit him in the head with a beer bottle."

My Hiawatha vision of India Joe was beginning to fade.

By then, Grandma, Papa, and I were tired. So, we had dinner in the lodge and got a good night's sleep. The next morning, we had breakfast in the lodge and went outside to enjoy the cool, clear weather. Saw a scruffy guy in khaki trousers and a khaki shirt walking toward us. He had greasy black hair and was probably about fifty. He had a stitched wound on his forehead. I was standing by Papa. Papa almost screamed, "Indian Joe." My Hiawatha vision was immediately deflated. But no worries. Indian Joe was the best Lac Seul fishing guide imaginable. He took us fishing every day in an outboard boat. We caught tons of northern pikes. He cooked them on the shore each day for lunch. The rest went back to the lodge for dinner. So beautiful. So wonderful. I plan on returning.

I was twenty-two and met many guys and gals my age around Ear Falls. Please understand, this is a sparsely populated, remote place. I partied with them in some of the few pubs in the area. In particular, I remember Rocky. Vietnam was raging and many Americans my age avoided the draft by fleeing to Canada, a sanctuary country with a no-deportation policy. Rocky was one of those guys. He had been in Canada a couple of years and had several businesses. He had a truck and started a garbage business. He had several customers: trailer homes, lodges, and a few businesses. Two or three times a week, Rocky and a friend of his made the garbage run and, of course, got paid. I made one of those garbage runs with them one day. Plus, Rocky had managed to get a boat and motor and was working as a fishing guide. We talked a lot. He knew I had been drafted and tried to convince me to stay in Canada. He assured me there was plenty of work to be had. But I had to decline. I believed I had a duty to my country to do what I had been called to do. As it turned out, January 21, 1977, President Jimmy Carter pardoned all Vietnam-era draft dodgers. I wonder whether Rocky stayed in Canada or returned to the US? Will never know.

After close to a week in Ear Falls, I caught a train to Winnipeg, boarded a connecting flight from there back to Houston, and attended my University of Houston graduation. After, September 8, 1969, I reported to the military induction center on San Jacinto Street in downtown Houston—the same center where, just a few years earlier, Cassius Clay

(Muhammed Ali) refused induction. The same day I reported I was on a bus to Fort Polk, Louisiana: quick processing, head shaved, gear issued, barracks assigned, and two months of "Army Strong."

CHAPTER 3
THE ARMY

The Private and the Colonel

MUST PREFACE THIS. Three things converged during July 1969: I worked Apollo 11 at NASA's Houston Manned Spacecraft Center as a public affairs protocol officer, finished my last course to graduate from the University of Houston, and received my draft notice. It was a confluence of life-changing events. When I received my draft notice, I told my boss that the Apollo 11 splashdown would be my last day at NASA. My plan before induction, which I fulfilled, was to drive my blue 1967 Mustang fastback from Houston to Isla Mujeres in the Yucatan. That's another story. Another factor was two of my University of Houston Pi Kappa Alpha fraternity brothers, Mike Driscoll and Dick Hancock.

After a couple of years in NASA's Manned Spacecraft Center Public Affairs Office, I had a pretty good reputation with my superiors and was able to bring these fellow fraternity brothers into my work group. They both had excellent pedigrees: Dick was an heir to the Hancock Oil & Gas Company; Mike was the nephew of Ralph Yarborough, the US Senate Majority Leader at the time. Mike was a Senate page and attended the Senate Page High School. During our college summers, he and Dick worked in Yarborough's Senate office in Washington. So, the story begins.

I reported to the military induction center on San Jacinto

Street in downtown Houston—the same center where, just a few years earlier, Cassius Clay (Muhammed Ali) refused induction. The same day I reported I was on a bus to Fort Polk, Louisiana: quick processing, head shaved, gear issued, barracks assigned, and two months of "Army Strong."

It was a hot October day at Fort Polk. I was about halfway through basic and my platoon was training in the hand-to-hand combat pit, a maybe fifty-by-eighty-foot pit outlined by railroad ties and filled with sawdust. We were there several days learning the intricacies of throwing enemy soldiers to the ground once you were out of ammo and your bayonet was useless. Glad I never had to face that moment. One day, a jeep driven by a lieutenant pulled up.

The lieutenant exited the jeep and walked over to my drill sergeant, sergeant Trimble, for a brief conversation. Next, sergeant Trimble called me out of the ranks. I moved through the pit and reported. Sergeant Trimble told me to get my gear and go with the lieutenant. I asked him what was up? But he didn't know. Dark clouds were forming on the horizon.

I collected my helmet, web gear, and M14 rifle and reported to the lieutenant with the proper salute. We got in the jeep and took off. I asked the lieutenant what was up, but he didn't know, except that he was supposed to take me to G2. I asked him what that was, and he informed me it was military intelligence (a contradiction in terms). So, we drove to post headquarters, which was right next to my company barracks. The lieutenant instructed me to go inside and report to Colonel so and so. I don't remember the colonel's name. The G2 building was one of those WWII, one-story, yellowish wood structures that were moved to our schools in the early fifties. Temporary "shacks" they were called then. I went in, set my helmet, web gear, and M14 by the wall and presented myself to a WAC at the nearest desk. "Private Luce reporting, ma'am." "Yes. We've been expecting you." She called a captain over and more salutes. The captain told me to follow him: "the Colonel's expecting you."

The colonel's office was right there, just a corner office of the small building. But the captain led me there and stood at attention as the colonel inspected me. More dark clouds. And it started. "Private Luce, there's a letter for you at the Fort Polk post office. It's from the US Senate. Do you know anything about that?" I didn't, but a vague thought began to form. "No sir." The colonel said, "Let's walk over to the post office," and led the captain and I out of G2.

It was a short walk to the post office, maybe two or three long blocks. My first mistake was walking to the right of the colonel. He snapped his fingers and motioned left. I had forgotten that I was supposed to walk to the left and half a step behind an officer. On the way to the post office, the colonel was quizzing me on what I thought about the war. What did I think about the anti-war movement? "I haven't thought about it sir." (Not true.) And we arrived at the post office.

The colonel, captain, and I walked in and went directly to a major sitting at his desk; he was up quickly and a salute. The colonel barked, "Major. This is private Luce. Do you have that letter?" "Yes sir." And the major moved to a large safe next to his desk. He worked the combination, turned the handle, and opened the safe. He reached inside and produced a thick envelope, which he handed to the colonel. The colonel looked at it for a second or two and handed it to me. I had the feeling he had seen it before. I held in my hands a letter in exquisite US Senate stationery and it was addressed to me. On the back of the envelope there was a security warning stamp, something to the effect that, "If you weren't authorized to read the letter, then you were in violation of this and that US law and subject to punishment including fines, imprisonment, and up to death." Not a good sign. Clouds were getting darker, but I had figured out that this was the probably alcohol-induced work of Dick and Mike. However, I was the one on the spot and had to think quickly. My action was to fold the letter in half and put it in the breast pocket of my fatigues. The colonel wasn't happy.

"Aren't you going to read the letter, Private Luce?"

"Yes sir. But later in my barracks."

"Private Luce, I would like for you to read it now."

Big decision time. I was thinking Leavenworth for me and maybe my dumb Pike brothers. How hard could I push? I took the envelope out of my pocket and opened it. The letter itself was the same luxurious US Senate stationery paper and had the same security warning on it. Great! And I began to read. Following is a short paraphrase because, as I will explain, the letter no longer exists.

"Dear Ray,

The Senator is encouraged by your reports of the treatment of our brave young men training at Fort Polk. The Senator reminds you to document your reports with dates and the names of individuals and witnesses involved. The Senator believes that your reports will assist him greatly in his effort to insure the fair treatment of those that have been called to serve. The Senator believes that your testimony before the Senate Armed Service Committee will be invaluable to his goal of ensuring proper treatment of our brave trainees. Having the power, we have the duty.

Sincerely,

Dick"

I didn't know where this was going to end but I decided to play the hand out. The colonel asked me, "What did the letter say?" I said, "Sorry sir. It's private and confidential." The colonel turned to the major and said, "Major, I want you to try and track this letter, and if you can find any violation of the law, I want charges brought." At that the colonel barked, "Private Luce, come with me." The colonel, captain, and I left the post office headed back to G2. On the way, the colonel asked me the same questions, "What do you think about the war? What do you think about the anti-war movement?" It seemed like a long walk back to G2.

When we arrived at G2, we went to the colonel's office. The colonel ordered me to sit in a chair next to his desk and put the captain at parade rest in front of his desk.

The colonel was direct: "Private Luce, I want to read that letter."

"I'm sorry sir, it's private and confidential."

"If I can't read the letter then we will have no alternative but to hold you suspect."

"Suspect of what, sir?"

"We won't know until after the investigation."

"What investigation, sir? I've been working at NASA the last three years and I have a secret security clearance."

"Private Luce, I know all about your background. But I promise you that our investigation will affect you for the rest of your military and civilian career. Now, I want to read that letter."

I was twenty-two years old. I was in a situation I could have never imagined. I had played the hand I had been dealt without betraying my dumb fraternity brothers. What was my hole card? And I played what I thought it might be. I knew the colonel wanted to read that letter more than anything in the world. So, I played the only hand I had.

"Sir, you can read the letter, but it has to be between you and me. You have to dismiss the captain."

"I wanted the captain here as a witness."

"I'm sorry, sir. It's private and confidential and has to be between you and me."

The colonel dismissed the captain, who came to attention, saluted, left, and closed the door. Now it was just me and the colonel. I took the letter out of my pocket, looked at it, and handed it to him. He didn't seem to be concerned about the "up to death" warning, opened the envelope, took the letter out, and read it. When he finished, it was one of those awkward who-speaks-first moments. It was him.

"Private Luce, you're nothing but a goddam spy." (Before I could respond.) "I guess you have your job to do and I have mine. What are you going to do with the letter?'

"Burn it, sir."

"Let's do that now."

The colonel grabbed his OD metal trash can and dumped the small amount of paper trash out of it, then he sat it down between us, reached in his pocket, and handed me a lighter. I was feeling better. The evidence would be destroyed. I took the lighter, lit the letter and envelope, and dropped them into the trash can. There, the private and the colonel sat watching the "Senator's" instructions go up in flames. And that was it; I was dismissed. But it wasn't over.

As I mentioned, my company barracks were located next to G2. I was the platoon guide for 2nd Platoon, which meant I ran the platoon under the guidance of Sergeant Trimble. One of 2nd Platoon's assignments was to police (pick-up trash and cigarette butts) around post headquarters each morning after breakfast. Thus, each morning I marched my platoon to headquarters and supervised the police. I was there the morning after the "letter incident" and the WAC I first met at G2 was just showing up for work and unlocking G2. My fight-or-flight instincts kicked in and I decided to fight—just in case.

I walked over to the WAC and said, "Pardon me ma'am. I was here yesterday."

"Oh, yes. You're that private."

I took my small notebook and pen out of my pocket—all basic trainees carry those—and asked, "What's your full name ma'am? What's the full name of the colonel I met yesterday?" I made my notes, thanked her and left. No doubt the colonel was duly informed.

A few weeks later, I graduated from basic training. All my company members received orders for their Advanced Individual Training (AIT) assignments—except me. "Houston. We have a problem." I spent the next two weeks working in the motor pool, changing tires and trying to figure out all the ways the colonel could have me killed, ruined, or worse. When my orders finally came through, I was assigned to armor training at Fort Knox, Kentucky. That was like winning the lotto. Armor (main battle tanks) meant almost a 100 percent chance of being sent to Europe, probably Germany, rather than Vietnam. Draftees didn't normally get assigned to armor, which was mostly reserved for enlistees. Fabulous. But disappointment is always just around the corner. After two months of training on those fifty-five-ton tanks, my AIT company graduated. Out of approximately two hundred troops, maybe a dozen of us were given orders to Vietnam. The colonel had a long reach. But it wasn't over, and Hancock and Driscoll weren't out of the picture.

I spent almost six months in a 9th Infantry Division mechanized infantry unit in Vietnam and Cambodia. After

Cambodia, Nixon announced troop withdrawals and the 9th was included. But there was a several months' delay, and I wanted to get off the line. I saw my chance in going to work for the 9th Infantry Division newspaper, *The Go Devil*, located about fifty miles south of Saigon at Tan An, a pretty scruffy place. I began to work that on my own but also wrote Hancock and Driscoll. They knew about the problem with the letter and the colonel and I told them they owed me. I told them to get off their asses and use their influence in Washington to get me off the line. I don't know whether it was my own actions or theirs that made it happen, but I ended up as a field correspondent working for *The Go Devil* newspaper. I rode helicopters out to units in the field, spent a couple of days with them, took pictures, returned to Tan An, and wrote my stories for publication in *The Go Devil*.

I had been in Tan An maybe two weeks when a captain looked me up. We exchanged salutes and he asked me, "Private Luce, are you happy?" Now that's either going to end up great or a disaster.

I answered, "Yes sir."

"Well, that's good. We got a 'Congressional inquiry' on you and I just wanted to follow-up and make sure everything is OK."

"Fine sir." And he left.

And the private is still here, without a criminal record, to recount this story.

The Reluctant Tunnel Rat

VILLAGES IN VIETNAM were under constant assault. Accordingly, every "hooch" in every village had a below-ground bunker, essentially a large, sandbag-covered foxhole below the hooch or just outside. When my platoon went into Cambodia, in May 1970, we realized it was the same there.

There were about four hundred soldiers in my unit, 2nd Battalion (mechanized) 47th Infantry Regiment, that actually crossed the border into Cambodia, and we traveled on maybe fifty to fifty-five armored personnel carriers (APC) and maybe a dozen trucks. I drove a two and a half ton truck, a "deuce and a half." After reaching the Cambodian border, some of the Battalion line units almost immediately entered Cambodia. The 2nd Battalion spent six-plus weeks in Cambodia. But different battalion units were on different schedules and for just over a week my platoon waited on the border. Finally, my platoon entered Cambodia May 9, returned to Vietnam May 15, reentered Cambodia May 21, and finally returned to Vietnam for good June 14. All in all, my platoon spent almost a month in Cambodia. During that period, we encountered many small Cambodian villages. I can't convey to you how primitive, by American standards, these villages were. But they were the homes of some great people and I was captivated by them and their grace. They weren't our enemies. Cambodia was neutral. But the Ho Chi Minh Trail went through Cambodia and we were there to interdict it. During the Cambodian campaign, the 2nd Battalion suffered seventy-eight casualties: twelve killed and sixty-six wounded, a twenty percent casualty rate.

As we encountered these villages, we had to "sweep" them (i.e., ensure there were no hostile troops or weapon/ military-supply caches). We were fighting North Vietnamese regular troops every day (mostly at night). Had to stay safe. One day we entered a bucolic village: very small, maybe a hundred villagers if that. Clear day. A few clouds. No rain. Mostly sunny. A few of our APCs and my truck pulled up in the center of the little village. The headman presented himself. All very cordial. He understood we had to sweep the village. I wasn't picking-up any bad vibes. So, we began our sweep. There was a below-ground covered trench, a tunnel, in the middle of the village and that's where the "reluctant tunnel rat" enters the picture.

There were a dozen or so of us armed American soldiers and all these unarmed Cambodian villagers. We were standing in a group in the middle of the village above an underground tunnel. My platoon sergeant, Sergeant Brunner, looked at me and ordered me to search the tunnel. It was one of those moments when you badly feel the need to pee.

From my perspective, I could see the contours of the tunnel from the surface. It was in the form of two right angles, like an open bracket: entrance and six-foot tunnel to the left, turn right and ten-foot tunnel straight and finally turn right and six-foot tunnel to exit. The tunnel was about four feet wide and four feet high; maybe the floor was six feet below surface. So, two feet of boards/earth/sandbags covering the tunnel. There was no light, except that seeping in from the entrances. I sucked it up and climbed into the tunnel with my fellow soldiers and the villagers watching.

It took a minute for my eyes to adjust. Was bright outside. Had my M16 on ready. Tunnel was only four-feet high so had to move through on my knees. First six feet, no problem. Peered around the first turn and still looked clear so made the turn. Just then, saw another person turning the corner, toward me, from the opposite end of the long leg of the tunnel. That's when training kicked in. America didn't send murderers to Vietnam. It sent its best and trained them well. But in a dark tunnel in a war zone your nerves are fragile. In an instant, I saw that this person had both hands on the ground—almost necessary to move through a four-foot-high tunnel, and I didn't perceive a weapon. We saw each other at about the same time. The light was very dim, but I waved him toward me. We crawled toward each other slowly in that dark tunnel. I had my M16 at the ready. When he got close, it turned out to be a kid about sixteen. I frisked him for a weapon and finding none indicated to him to pass me and leave the tunnel. Heart racing now to the point of bursting. But not out of the tunnel yet.

I moved to the end of the long section of tunnel and carefully peeked around the turn. There was better light there because it was near the exit, and "boom," another person. Could tell immediately this person was female and young. She appeared unarmed. So, M16 still at the ready, I motioned for her to exit the tunnel. I followed her out.

The scene above ground was surreal: all the villagers, the American soldiers I was with, the boy I encountered in the tunnel and could have killed, the headman (the boy's father), the girl (daughter of another prominent villager I believe), and a general, foreboding sense of what's next?

As it turns out, the young guy and girl just happened to be making out in the tunnel when my platoon rolled into the village. We moved in quickly—call it "combat speed." I found them and, because of me, their dalliance was discovered by their parents. The young guy and girl probably hated me for that. But it could have been a lot worse—surely for them, and definitely for me. If I had pulled the trigger in that dark tunnel, don't know whether I could have ever lived with myself.

Think about what I have told you here. It's very difficult for the young men and women we send to fight for us to know what to do, with just an instant to decide, when they are faced with life-or-death decisions. We should never second-guess them, nor should our leaders.

Ray W. Luce on Cambodian Border.

2nd Battalion is convoying into Cambodia.

Cambodian villagers waving at the 2nd Battalion.

Ray W. Luce hanging out with a young Cambodian.

Sergeant Bruner, who ordered Ray W. Luce to search the tunnel.

A Week in a MASH Unit

AFTER MY MECHANIZED infantry unit left Cambodia in 1970, the army eventually parked us near Bearcat northeast of Saigon. We were there for over a month. One day, a Tuesday, while stringing concertina wire in front of our position I scratched my left wrist on the wire. Woke up Wednesday morning with an itch at the scratch. By noon, a red streak was running up my arm. Just happened that sick call was Wednesday. A doc came in by jeep from Bearcat every Wednesday; had an armed troop driving him. Lined up for sick call. When my turn came, told him what happened and showed him my arm. He said, "You're going back to Bearcat with me."

In Bearcat, I was put into a sandbagged Mobile Army Surgical Hospital (MASH) unit and hooked up to an antibiotic IV drip. Spent a week in bed there. Was feeling fine but had a life-threatening infection. I made friends with some of the medics. Their hooch was next to the MASH unit. In the evenings they invited me to come visit with them, which I did. They led me to their hooch as I held my IV drip over my head. In their hooch, I just hung it on a nail and we listened to music from the World (a general reference to the life we left behind in the US) on their tape players. It was a rare, restful week.

Unfortunately, some badly wounded guys cycled through that facility. Felt terrible for them.

But even in the field hospital, couldn't escape the war. Accordingly, there was a sandbagged entrance on each end of the MASH structure built in right angles so, if a mortar or rocket round came in, shrapnel would not penetrate to the patient area. One night, the base was penetrated by VC sappers. They threw a satchel charge at the MASH unit. When I heard the explosion I wanted my M16, but the armorer took it away from me when I checked in. Due to all the sandbagging and right angles, the hospital was fine, and there were plenty of healthy US Army troops outside to take care of the sappers.

The Go Devil

AFTER THE CAMBODIAN invasion, in August 1970, I transitioned from my 2nd Battalion (mechanized) 47th Infantry Regiment to the 9th Infantry Division newspaper, *The Go Devil*. I was a field correspondent, essentially a combat news reporter. I rode Huey helicopters out to units in the field, took photos, and wrote an accompanying story for publication. On one occasion, I spent two days and a night with Company B, 5th Battalion, 60th Infantry Regiment. Spent the night with them in a dry rice paddy wrapped in a poncho. Didn't take my M16, only a sidearm, a .45-caliber Colt 1911. As it turned out, that was OK. We weren't hit. All in all, it was a close-up glimpse of the day-to-day life of an army infantry "grunt."

Of course, the Huey I rode on to Company B had an M-60 door gunner onboard, one of Vietnam's icons. Vietnam was the rice bowl of Asia. On the way to join Company B, I flew over endless miles of fertile rice paddies. But, eventually, we flew over areas that had been bombed by B-52s. It was so sad to see the meticulously tended land rendered asunder by modern weapons of destruction. These fields were the villages' center of life for untold generations. Ultimately, we flew over heavily carpet-bombed fields.

Carpet bombing is an abstract term, unless you were the target of it. I've been close to the resulting craters, close enough to feel the earth shake during the drop ("rolling thunder"). The earth is soft and the bombs are massive. The resulting craters can easily be fifty feet across and twenty feet deep and many fill up with water. I have been swimming in them. I've set up in a dry crater, with my unit, for ambush purposes. Good idea, except the one my unit set up in had CS gas canisters at the bottom, which seeped up during the night and wreaked havoc on our eyes— long night. These were bucolic villages surrounded by their rice. I can't imagine this in my neighborhood.

As my Huey approached Company B, I had a great view from the air of the unit I would spend the next two days with. They had been on ambush the night before and were in their "day hold" position until time to move to another ambush position in the evening. Vietnam was hot. It was amazing how these guys improvised some shade, using ponchos and poncho liners, to at least ameliorate the heat of the sun. The Huey landed, dropped me off, and left.

I met the Company Commander and began taking pictures for publication in *The Go Devil*, along with my story copy. The soldiers I interviewed didn't want to be there but, like me, they felt a duty to the country. During the day, these guys tried to get some rest. But in the combat zones, things were always blowing up. There were huge explosions: some from artillery, some from bombs, some from troops blowing ordinance in place because they could not carry it all. We always had more ammunition then we needed—no complaints there. Some of that was going on close enough to make sleep in the daytime more difficult.

In the afternoon, a Huey approached the landing zone

(LZ), smoke was popped, and it was guided in. This Huey was bringing a hot meal and mail to the platoon. It meant a lot to them. After chow was over, the empty food containers were loaded onboard and the Huey left. So, it was time to get down to business: preparing for a long "hump" (a hike) and setting-up an ambush position. Weapons had to be cleaned and checked. Ammo had to be distributed. Map coordinates had to be confirmed. And guts had to be checked.

These soldiers carried a heavy load: pack with supplies, weapons, ammo, radios, water, and much more. The radios were our lifelines. Middle of nowhere. Dependent on resupply for everything. Dependent on artillery or air support in a firefight. All the foregoing dependent on our radios. We depended a lot on the radios and our officers. We respected our officers because most were good guys. Also, in the scenario described here, they were right there with us. More, they were the only guys that knew where we were. They could call in the Hueys for food and resupply. They could call in the medevacs. They could call in artillery or air support. They were indispensable.

I had been in a mechanized infantry unit; never had to walk. So, it was enlightening to "hump" five to ten "klicks' (kilometers) with these guys. They were carrying weapons, ammo, radios, and other heavy gear; I only had a camera, sidearm, and light pack. It was a long, late-afternoon walk through the paddies.

The 5th of the 60th was in Cambodia with the rest of us in the 9th Infantry Division. They cleared and landed at LZ "Shakey's Hill," which was their Cambodian home from June 1 through 26, 1970. Their major accomplishment was finding and evacuating one of the most significant caches of the Cambodian operation. They captured fourteen individual and thirteen crew-served weapons and evacuated 33.4 tons of rice and 220 pounds of medical supplies. They discovered 150 tons of enemy ammunition. The 5/60 killed twenty-four enemy but suffered two killed and fifteen wounded. And these soldiers were still in the fight here.

During the hump, we saw several villagers working the rice paddies. Out in the "boonies," Vietnam is a village-oriented, rice-growing society. It is so sad that the war was raging around them while all they wanted to do was grow their rice, worship their ancestors, and love their family.

I spent the night in the ambush position—a dry rice paddy. It didn't rain, but I slept wrapped-up in my poncho. No mosquitos, but every other crawling bug you can imagine kept me company. I only had my .45 but I felt safe. I was surrounded by almost forty heavily armed soldiers that I had just spent the day with, all of us, me included, in a situation we never imagined.

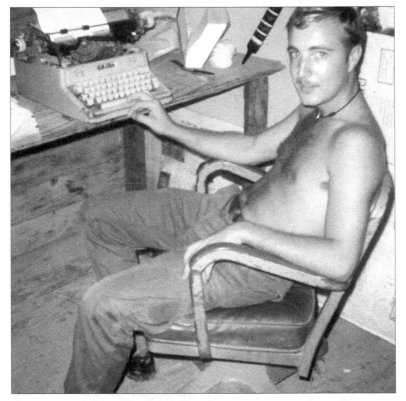

Ray W. Luce at his desk with typewriter at
The Go Devil, **Tan An, Vietnam.**

*Ray W. Luce rode this Huey to join Company B
in their day hold position.*

The Huey flew over endless, carefully tended rice paddies.

Ariel view of rice paddies subjected to carpet bombing.

B Company soldiers cleaning weapons under homemade shade.

Soldier has popped smoke and is guiding in Huey bringing hot chow to B Company.

B Company moving out to set up their night ambush position.

Villagers tending their rice with water buffalo.

Take a Stripe and Send Him to Gia Nghia

THIS IS A story about what could have happened to an honorable soldier that unintentionally mishandled classified information. In the end, it worked out OK for me but could have resulted in a prison sentence.

After my unit withdrew from Cambodia, Nixon announced withdrawals from Vietnam and the 9th Infantry Division was on the list. There were about ten thousand of us. It took months for the ultimate withdrawal of the 9th and, in the end, it was just a normal rotation, a single planeload of 9th Infantry Division troops returning to Ft. Lewis, Washington, with the colors of the 9th. The rest of us were redeployed in country—good example of government lies. From withdrawal from Cambodia in the spring of 1970 until the 9th was dispersed in the fall of 1970 was about five months. During those five months, knowing almost all of us were not going home (yet . . . and for some, never), it was every man for himself. And I took the initiative.

To keep the story short, I took successful steps to transfer from my mechanized infantry unit to the 9th Infantry Division newspaper, *The Go Devil.* The mechanized unit wasn't in the fight anymore anyway; just waiting for what redeployment meant resulted in a lot of guys just sitting around, some doing drugs. Didn't need that. So, I made it to *The Go Devil* and spent a few months with a camera and typewriter flying out to 9th Infantry Division troops that were still in the fight, taking pictures and writing copy for *The Go Devil* publication. But, *The Go Devil* was still the 9th and, when the final dispersion happened, it would be dissolved.

As part of my *The Go Devil* job, every couple of weeks I flew on an Air America (CIA airline operation in Vietnam) flight (six or eight seats on a tail dragger) to Saigon. *The Go Devil* editor and I took our latest copy to the *Stars and Stripes* (the official countrywide army newspaper publication) to have our type set and newspapers printed to distribute to the ten thousand 9th Infantry Division troops. So, I knew the *Stars and Stripes* staff, enlisted and officer.

Just prior to withdrawal of the 9th, I convinced my first sergeant to issue bogus orders for me to transfer to Saigon, assigned to the *Stars and Stripes*, part of the Military Assistance Command Vietnam (MACV). I went, reported to the officers I had met, and was accepted. I was safe in the MACV compound in Saigon. But I hated it: all lifer crap, all spit and polish. No understanding what the real fight was like. It was unbearable for a free spirit who had been in the fight. Luckily, after a couple of weeks, my "real" orders showed up. I was being assigned as a security guard at Ben Tuan, some godforsaken outpost on the fringes of the war. I had a decision to make. I was confident I could stay in Saigon or risk it again at Ben Tuan. I took the risk.

I caught an army transport plane from Saigon to Nha Trang. Nha Trang was a beautiful, old French resort on the South China Sea. There was a big US air base at Nha Trang.

After landing, I was transferred to the Civil Operations and Rural Development Support (CORDS) compound a few miles from the air base. CORDS was the CIA operation in Vietnam and is best known for the Phoenix assassination program conducted before I arrived. The CORDS compound was located in an old French hotel a block off a beautiful beach. The main building and rooms were used for an office facility and bungalows in the back quarters for officers. Perfect. Beautiful. Why would you leave here to go to Ben Tuan?

I was prepared. I had put together a resume. I used a 9th Infantry Division Promotional piece for the front and back covers. I had my college graduate records and letters sent from my family and friends in Houston. Many were from my NASA bosses and people I had taken on tours there as a NASA Protocol Officer. There were pictures of me with astronauts taking VIPs on tours of the Manned Spacecraft Center. There was a work order for me to handle the director of NASA on one of his visits to our center. It was all three-hole punched and bound with grenade pull-rings (nice touch for a combat veteran). It was twenty-plus pages in all and I still have it.

When I met with the sergeant that was going to assign me to Ben Tuan, I asked him if there were any jobs there at the CORDS headquarters. He said a few and I pulled out my resume. He flipped through it and asked me to wait. He left. Ten or fifteen minutes later a major, Philip Perles, came back with the sergeant. Major Perles was the new signal officer for II Corps in Vietnam, and he needed a clerk. A clerk in the army that could type was rare. A clerk that could type, had a college degree, already had a secret clearance from NASA, had three-plus years' experience in NASA Protocol, and a great resume was determinative. Better pedigree than most officers. Major Perles hired me on the spot.

So, I ended up helping Major Perles run signal for II Corps. We regularly published the signal operation instructions (SOI) for the MACV teams in the field. Big deal. We had a large safe in our office and daily handled confidential signal information. At the end of each day, we put all confidential documents to be destroyed in a brown paper grocery bag and took it to a central security office in the compound to be burned that day. Routine. Then one day, I signed out a top-secret (my clearance level) document from that office.

I was a combat troop—an armored (tank) crewman to be precise, but I ended up with the 47th Infantry Regiment/9th Infantry Division in a mechanized infantry unit. I was trained on a lot of weapons, but I was not trained on how to handle classified documents, and I received no training from CORDS. So, I had signed out this top-secret document. It had all the call signs and frequencies for all US leadership in Vietnam, both civilian and military. Major Perles and I needed it for our work. I had never handled a top-secret document before. At the end of the day, I put it in a confidential burn bag as usual. But before the offices closed that evening the sergeant who ran the security office found me and asked for the document. I was supposed to have signed it back in, but it was in a burn bag. He freaked and immediately reported the incident to the colonel we all worked for. Good guy, but he was pissed. Probably figured I would be the last guy to screw up like that. His judgment, "Take a Stripe and send him to Gia Nghia." As it turned out, the burn bags were still safe in the security office. We went through them until the top-secret document was located. So, there was no way it was compromised. And the colonel, major, and sergeant were happy about that. No blemishes on them. I was happy too. Didn't have to go to Gia Nghia and, probably therefore, I'm alive to recount this story.

Some politicians seem to be immune, but one inadvertent mistake on the part of a loyal American soldier could have threatened his entire life. Handling classified information is serious business.

CHAPTER 4
LETTERS HOME FROM THE FRONT

13JUL45

My Dad, Wilbert R. Luce, served in the Navy during WWII along with two of his brothers, Dave and Fred. From Dad's written memoirs, following is the route his ship, The Livingston, took through the western Pacific: Tarawa, Eniwetok, Kwajalein, Russell Islands, Guadalcanal, Espirito Santo, Noomea New Caledonia, Ulithi, Okinawa, Peleliu, Guam, Saipan, Iwo Jima, Tokyo Bay, and final victory. Hard men, with hard bark, fighting a hard war. They were the "greatest generation." Below is a letter home from Dad to his mom, dad, and youngest brother, Bob.

W. R. Luce - Rd. M. 2/c   6 CENTS AIR MAIL
U. S. S. Livingston - AK222   U. S. NAVY, JUL 13, 1945
c/o - F.P.O. - San Francisco, Cal.

Mr. and Mrs. D. R. Luce and Bob
321 East 20th Ave.
Houston, 8, Texas

PASSED BY NAVAL CENSOR, A.S.M.

Thursday 7:30 P.M. - July 12, 1945

Dear folks,

Don't remember exactly when or what I wrote last, but I decided to write anyway, and let you know I'm rocking along just waiting to get home one of these days.

Boy a change of weather always made me sick with a cold; so I don't know how I'll make out the way we are circling around now. Feels pretty cool to me now after the hot weather we've been in recently.

Guess Norma Lee told you by now of my experience crossing the equator. I wouldn't want that initiation regular. It is rather annoying, but humorous to look back on!

Mother we all enjoyed the picture folder of San Antonio which arrived today, and we from that vicinity sure wish we were around there now.

Mother I write midnight letters around here, but I was surprised that you did the same. Glad to hear from you anyway.

Guess you and Bob enjoyed your visit with Vera in spite of the difficulties.

Glad you are enjoying a bit of watermelon. Norma Lee was telling me they had cantaloupe at fourteen cents a pound.

Sorry now I didn't at least write you Father's Day Dad, but I did think of you and had written Norma Lee to do something for you, but I guess she didn't get my letter in time.

Wish I were around to help you at the store Dad. Hope you don't work too hard. You need to play more. As you said always life is too short to miss the pleasant things. I know you've always liked your work, but you should get away from it more.

Afraid I've lost some of this worldwide desire for money. The big thing I want now is just to get along and be happy and that won't take much after being in this mess for a couple of years.

Bob I hope you have that cap from Norma Lee by now. I have another for you now.

I have written both Dave and Fred lately and am waiting to hear from them. Sure hope Fred has a nice visit home in August before he ships out. Wonder what Dave will do?

Had a mid-watch last night and need a little rest; so I guess I'll close now. Seeing new scenery, but I can't go into detail. Bye for now.

Bert

Author's note: Unlike the rest of this book, the following letters were transcribed from the handwritten originals without edit, except for a few items: the formatting was adjusted, spelling was corrected, and a few personal lines were omitted.

3MAR70

Dear Mom & Dad,

I left Oakland Thursday and arrived in Bien Hoa, Vietnam Saturday. It was a long flight, and we stopped at Hawaii and Okinawa to refuel. I was bussed 9 miles from Bien Hoa to Long Ben where I spent one day with the 90th replacement battalion. Yesterday I was shipped to Tan An Airstrip. It's a little landing strip in the center of a small compound. There are about 400 people here. Tan An is located in the Mekong Delta. I spent all last night on perimeter defense. There was fighting all around from dark till dawn, explosions, rifle shots, and illumination flares. This compound is pretty well fortified, and hasn't been hit in a couple of months, so last night we just watched and listened, but nothing happened. In about a week I'll be assigned to my final destination, a unit somewhere out in the field.

I'm putting $125.00 per month in a 10% savings plan that pays quarterly. That plus my bond makes me saving $150.00 per month.

I'll write again soon. You write our representatives and tell them to get everybody out of here. Say hello to Kenneth, and tell him I'll write soon.

Love,
Ray

PS: Don't use the address on the envelope. When you do get my final address I want you to mail me that leather belt I had made and a high-quality hunting knife. The knife should be dark colored (blue steel) nothing that would show up or shine. I'll need a whetstone too.

9MAR70

Dear Mom & Dad,

I finally reached my unit where I'll be till it's time to come home. I'm in the 9th Infantry Division about 50 miles south of Saigon near the town of Binh Phuoc. I'm in the headquarters company of a mechanized infantry unit. I'm in what they call a "Flame." We operate light armored vehicles fitted with a huge flame thrower rather than a main gun. I'll tell you more about what we do after I've been here a while. Today is my first day.

You can't imagine the living conditions here. It's hot and dirty and there are no conveniences at all. I'll tell you more about this compound later but it will take me a few days to look it over.

I'm putting $125.00 per month into a 10% Army savings plan, plus my $20.00 bond. It all comes out of my paycheck before I even see it. If I have any extra out of the money I keep, I'll send it to you.

I have an address now, so I would like to hear from you. Send me the knife I need and the belt I had made (don't forget the little loop). Let me know how everybody is doing and tell them I'll write as soon as I get settled. I really miss you; I hope you are both well and happy.

Love,
Ray

P.S. It's just getting dark and I can already hear the fighting. I don't think I'll ever get used to the noise.

PFC Ray W. Luce
HHC 2nd/47th
9th Div.
APO S.F. 96371
Flame Platoon

GOD SAID LET THERE BE LIGHT AND THERE WAS "LLUMO"

14MAR70

Dear Mom & Dad,

Well I'm getting settled down now. I live in a big bunker made out of 8″ x 8″ timbers and covered & surmounted with sand-bags. It's like sleeping in a basement. We went out burning the last two days. Yesterday we used 1,800 gallons of napalm. You should see the tanks fire; it's really pretty.

When you write me, send me some U of H basketball clip-pings. Don't forget my belt and knife too. Say hello to Grandma and Papa & tell them I'll write soon. I'll write more later but I have to go to work now.

Love,
Ray

24MAR70

Dear Mom & Dad,

I thought I would write and tell you about a battle I watched last night. There are four companies of about 150 men each in our compound. There is Headquarters Company that I'm in, Alpha, Bravo and Charlie companies. Well Charlie Company went out yesterday evening and just after dark they got into some really heavy contact with a North Vietnamese unit. I watched the whole battle from a guard tower; it lasted about two hours. First there was an artillery and mortar salvo fired in support from our position. It's really weird; first you hear the boom of the artillery and mortar pieces, they you can hear the shells like jet planes heading for the target and then you hear the explosions in the distance. There were 3 or 4 flares in the air over the battle zone all of the time. I could hear Charlie company's 50 caliber machine guns firing and could see the tracers ricocheting up into the air. Then the helicopter gunships moved in. I could see the lights on the choppers, three or four of them flying at about 2000 feet. Then the gunships opened up with rockets and mini-guns. It was just a stream of red pouring from several different points in the sky, but all concentrated at one point on the ground. It was cool last night and I sat in an easy chair in the breeze and watched the fighting. It was exciting and really pretty to watch the flares and tracers, but I really felt sorry for the guys in Charlie Company. They had one man killed and seven badly wounded; we haven't heard the enemy body count. I'm really worried about what I'll do when my platoon makes contact. It's really frightening when you think about fighting like that out in the dark of night.

I thought you might like to know about the troop withdrawals too. Nixon tells you that the 1st division's 50,000 men have been pulled out, and they have. Actually, when the division left, only 400 went home. 49,600 men were reassigned in country. For instance, several hundred were sent to our base. The troop withdrawals are a joke and the idea of turning the war over to the South Vietnamese is a joke too. Believe me, all of the things we were hearing when I was still home were either out and out lies, half-truths, or nothing was said at all. If our leaders were straight forward with you, then they would tell you that our troop strength is as big here as ever, and they would admit that a lot of us or other soldiers still at home will soon be in Laos. I wish you would believe that what the anti-war movement has been talking about for the last 11 years (that's how long we've been here) is true and right, and you would use whatever influence you have over anyone you know to help bring this disaster to a close. There just isn't any sense in having any more Bob Mcintyres. I think it's gone on for so long that people just don't care anymore, but apathy will cost a lot of young lives.

All in all I'm doing alright only I haven't gotten any mail yet. I really miss hearing from you. I know you love me but wish I could hear you say it in a letter. I hope I get a letter tomorrow. Well have to go to sleep now. Tell Grandma and Papa I miss them, and say hello to Kenneth for me. I love you and think about you and all the good things we did together over the years. I wish I knew how to thank you for everything.

Love,
Ray

10APR70

Dear Mom & Dad,

I received my tapes today and they really are great. You really have made me happy. Please thank Tom and Sherry for me. You asked about the model numbers of my tape player and radio. The radio is a Sony 7F-81W and the tape player is a Panasonic RQ-209S. I'm listening to my tapes right now and Indian Jo is recording them for his player. You should have the $60.00 I sent for the tapes by now. Send *Surrealistic Pillow, Crown of Creation* and *After Bathing at Baxters* as soon as you can. The food package came today too. I already ate all of the Sesame sticks.

Our Battalion is leaving Binh Phuoc in four or five days. We're moving north of Saigon and we really will be out in the boonies. There won't be any electricity (I bought two cases of radio batteries yesterday), no bunkers to live in and in general nothing but what we can carry in our tracks. We're only allowed to take TO&E equipment with us; that is just what we need to fight with. We loaded all of our napalm into the trailers today and I'm packing my bags. The guys that have been here a while have to mail most of their personal things home or just walk off and leave them. My radio and tape player are the only extra things I'm taking with me. We have to use highway #4 through Saigon to reach our new area of operation. It will really be a sight to see a whole mechanized Battalion moving in convoy. There will be hundreds of tracks and trucks so the convoy will stretch for miles. I hate to leave because it's a lot of trouble and the fighting is a lot heavier in the north.

You asked about my friends here. In the flame platoon there is Indian Jo. He's a crazy Sioux. He doesn't have to cut his hair because he's an Indian so he's letting it grow down to his tukus. John Self is my best friend. He's from a whiskey running area in Tennessee. He really lived the Thunder Road life and he even looks like Robert Mitcham. Topliff is another wild guy. He rode with the Angels in L.A. and he really is tough. He's missing some teeth and has a real interesting tattoo. The sergeants are scared of him but we're good friends. They took him off the machine gun because the V.C. were able to identify him and put a bounty on him. They say he was as good as a whole platoon when he was working out with his machine gun. He's killed a lot of V.C. The only other really close friend I have is a surfer from San Diego. His name is Leslie (Sam) Stevens. I call him Giant because he's 6'6" and he looks like John Wayne. He's in the recon platoon. A few nights ago recon made contact and killed two V.C. I asked him what there was to do for fun around here when I first met him and he just smiled and said "Kill V.C."

I had a chance to go to sniper school but I turned it down. Some of the snipers have 60 or 70 kills and a lot of them are really cold blooded. Snipers have to register with law enforcement agencies when they return to civilian life.

Be sure and let me know when the $100.00 check I sent you arrives. I'm writing Kenneth today to let him know I sent him $50.00. I may send him my tape player and buy another one for myself. Let me know how my car is doing when you write and put a tape in your player every now and then just to exercise it. You should listen to it all the time. Go to Foleys and buy some tapes you enjoy. Use the $50.00 I sent you. Well that's all for now. Write soon.

Love,
Ray

20APR70

Dear Mom & Dad,

I'm at Cu Chi now. A couple of days before the 2/47 was planned to move they sent me to a ten-day combat leadership course. I'll be back with the 2/47 in about five days. I don't know where they are now but they should be north of Saigon by now.

This school is pretty interesting. We're learning how to use demolition equipment, how to call in artillery, how to call in gunships and medevacs, and many other things. The only thing bad about the school is that Cu Chi is a big base and there are lots of lifers around. Also, I have to wait until I get back to my unit to get any mail. When you write, let me know where Grandma and Papa are so I can write them. There isn't much to talk about now. Cu Chi is pretty quiet. It's awfully hot though. The last day of the school we have to go out on a night ambush patrol, but I doubt if we'll see anything.

It seems like the time just drags on. The only thing I have to look forward to before I come home is my R&R. I may go to Hong Kong and buy some stereo equipment and clothes. I have a lot of time to think about that though. Mostly I'm looking forward to catching that freedom bird back to the world.

My watch finally gave out on me; it was a good one I guess because it lasted six years. I'll have to buy another one. The watches here are pretty cheap at least.

I sure wish I could have been at NASA for Apollo 13. I really missed a lot of excitement but at least I was there for the first landing. I'm looking forward to going back to my old job. Will write again soon.

Love,
Ray

27APR70

Dear Mom & Dad,

Your letter came yesterday telling me that Papa has left us. I was so lonely last night; there wasn't anyone here to share my sadness with. All I could think of was that Grandma said Papa didn't plant a garden this year in one of her letters. Papa loved his garden and I know God loved Papa for using the Earth the way it was meant to be used. I guess when he looked down and saw that the little patch of ground Papa use to love was old and didn't bloom this spring that it was time to call the gardener home. I'm so sad. I just think of him and the oil rigs and what a treat is was to have him with us on Christmas when I was little. Just before I left he said the ducks would be following in front of his 12 gauge when I got back. There won't be anyone to clean my ducks for me now.

I went to Long Ben today to try and call but I couldn't. I want to see you and Grandma so bad. Maybe she would like to meet me in Hawaii for my R&R. If I could spend a week with her in that beautiful place, maybe it would make her happy. I loved Papa so much. He was my Papa. I named him. I hope they called him Papa at the funeral. Please write me and tell me how everyone is. I'm sorry I'm so far away. Make sure Kay knows and ask her to call Grandma for me. I'm so sad. I wish I could be with all of you.

Love,
Ray

2MAY70_1

Dear Mom and Dad,

I hope my letters reach you quicker than your mail gets to me. The mail I've been getting has been two weeks old. We convoyed the 17th of last month to Bearcat above Saigon, and stayed there about 5 or 6 days. I slept on a piece of plywood there. We began dropping off unnecessary equipment there. Then we convoyed to Tay Ninh which is farther north and about 8 miles from Cambodia. I slept on a cement floor there for the 2 nights we stopped there. At least I was dry. We left everything at Tay Ninh except essential items like a change of clothes, poncho, etc. We also were supplied with huge loads of ammunition. Day before yesterday we convoyed to the border above the parrot beak that Nixon mentioned. The next morning our infantry units crossed into Cambodia. About 2 hours later Nixon spoke and while we listened over a hundred choppers loaded with troops flew overhead for the other side of the border. A few hours later they started bringing prisoners and captured weapons into our perimeter. The armor units that were with us crossed the border this morning. Once the NVA base camps are located and secured I imagine the flame will cross to burn them down. So far, the 2nd & 47th hasn't suffered any battle deaths.

I've been wet almost all of the time. I slept in a puddle of water last night until I had to move. I crawled under a trailer and slept pretty good the rest of the night. There are swarms of bees and flying ants here too, and they drive you crazy. We have plenty of food but it's all canned C rations. Whenever I get home I'm going to have a house with a picture window facing the back yard, and I'm going to build a sandbag bunker back there. Then whenever things aren't going well I'll just sit back in an easy chair and remember that things could be a lot worse.

I received a letter from Charlie yesterday; he sent me a picture of the baby and one of my going away party. They are really nice pictures. Write soon; I'll write when I can.

Love,
Ray

2MAY70_2

Dear Uncle Dave,

I guess things haven't changed much since you were in the service. Ever since I've been in the Army I've been either hot and tired, wet and tired, or cold and tired. Now I'm hot and tired in the daytime, cold and tired at night, and wet all of the time. I have C rations running out of my ears too. Right now I'm sitting on the Cambodian border. I've been here 3 days and 2 nights. Yesterday our infantry units crossed the border early in the morning. By yesterday afternoon they were bringing back prisoners and captured weapons. I don't know if the flame will cross or not. They may not want us to burn the enemy base camps after they have been taken.

I heard my Papa had died, but we're moving so fast I haven't had much time to really think about that. I was really sad and lonely when I heard the bad news.

I'm sending you a picture of my best friend here and some things you might enjoy reading. Write when you can and say hello to your family for me.

Love,
Ray

4MAY70

Dear Mom and Dad,

Today is Monday; I wouldn't have known except the medics passed the pink malaria pills that we take every Monday. We're still sitting on the border waiting to find out what's going to happen next. Yesterday I had to help two other guys escort eight prisoners to the makeshift airstrip we have for shipment to the rear. Three of them were North Vietnamese soldiers, three were V.C., and two were old, old Cambodians. The N.V.A. soldiers had their hands tied, but the others didn't. That's the first time I ever had to hold a weapon on another human being. When the prisoners looked at me it sent shivers down my back. They were pretty peaceful and did what we indicated without arguing; I was glad of that.

I sent a roll of slides to Kodak to be developed, and they will mail them to you. The pictures if they come out are of our position here on the border, a captured Chinese machine gun, and some of the prisoners.

Your care package came yesterday. I'm glad you sent the maple sugar. I also like the sesame sticks you've been sending.

Charlie wrote and sent me a picture of the baby, and a picture of the family at grandma Luce's house from my going away party. Papa is in the pictures so it really pleased me. My friends at N.A.S.A. sent me a packet of pictures, and everyone enjoyed them.

Carol is getting ready to graduate so buy her a present for me and I'll send some money when I get paid. I haven't been paid for last month yet. I'm glad my car is almost paid for; I'll try to send money for the last couple of payments.

I'll write again soon, but I'm almost out of paper. Don't worry about me; I feel pretty safe where I am now. About all we worry about is a mortar attack, and we've finished building some sturdy bunkers so that doesn't even bother us now. Write soon and say hello to everyone.

Love,
Ray

5MAY70

Dear Mom and Dad,

Well I'm still just sitting here on the border, and it's getting pretty boring. We had a little excitement last night. We had what we call a mad minute. Just to make sure the enemy knows we're ready we occasionally open up with every weapon we have around our perimeter. We opened up last night with 50 cals., m 60s, 16s, 79s, mortars, and rockets. It was just a firepower display but it was really exciting. Tracers really are pretty at night. I fired a couple of magazines.

Last night I was on guard and Indian Jo was sitting in front of me. Another guy was sitting beside me facing Jo. Our Company Commander was on the other side of me. It was real dark and then someone popped some illumination. The guy next to me said, "Look out Jo a snake!" Jo jumped away just before it struck. The Captain and I tried to pin its head down but it kept striking at us and then it jumped 2 feet. That's when we decided to shoot it. I blew it in half with a couple of shots. Poor Indian Jo really has it tough. A couple of nights ago he slid into his sleeping bag and his bare feet ran right in into another snake coiled in the bottom of his bag. He doesn't sleep in the bag anymore. In fact it's right where he left it. He said he wasn't going to argue with the snake.

Our dog, Spook, made the trip from Binh Phuoc to here with us and he's been sleeping with me. He's always sniffing around my sleeping area so I don't worry too much about the snakes. Well that's all for now. Write soon.

Love,
Ray

10MAY70

Dear Mom and Dad,

First, I want to wish you a happy Mother's Day Mom. I hope Dad and Kenneth do something nice for you. I'm sorry I can't send you anything.

Yesterday morning, we moved into Cambodia. We went through the thickest jungle you've ever seen. A couple of tanks led the convoy and they made a path through the jungle for everyone behind them. The tracks made it pretty well, but the trucks keep getting stuck and had to be pulled out of the mud over and over again. I drive a 2½ ton truck and I didn't get stuck once. The driving I did in Yucatan really was good experience for here. Well, we finally broke out of the jungle into some of the prettiest country I've ever seen. Cambodia is red dirt country like Woodville or Tyler. We drove through miles and miles of beautiful villages. The houses were all on stilts and everything was well taken care of. The villagers, peasants, lined the road in front of their houses. There were over a thousand in all at least. We're the first Americans they have ever seen and they really seemed pleased. Every one of them from the youngest to the oldest waved, and clapped, and smiled. They acted like they were really glad to see us. I took pictures and I hope they come out. You can tell there's been no war here. The people are much nicer looking and healthier than the Vietnamese, and their clothes are more colorful and primitive.

We stopped to rest last night, and in a few minutes we're leaving again. We're going to move toward Cambodia's capital city, but I don't know if we'll enter it or not. Somewhere between here and there we expect to find the NVA. It's a shame the war has to be brought to this beautiful place. I'm afraid the people won't be smiling when we drive back through those villages returning to Vietnam.

At least we all have one thing to be glad about; we're not in Vietnam anymore. You can really be proud of all the guys here. They've gone without hot food, clean clothes, a place to sleep other than a hole in the earth, anything to drink except water, and any other simple luxury you can think of for almost a month. They've endured lots of hardship and some of them have lost good friends, but they just keep smiling and do what has to be done. When we hear about all of the trouble at home we just shake our heads because we don't understand.

What impresses me is that for any person at home you can find a duplicate of him here. Some of the guys here are just as radical as the ones at home on the university campuses. For every boozer at home there's one here and he probably drinks more. For every pot head at home there's one here and he probably smokes more. The difference is that the ones here are doing their duty and they are suffering a lot in the process. When all the guys from the Nam come home I think they will be the leaders that will keep the country going. Well I have to go now. Write when you can.

Love,
Ray

13MAY70

Dear Mom and Dad,

It will be a while before I'm able to mail this or any of the letters I've been writing. We've been in Cambodia close to a week now, and it's been like a vacation. The first few days we moved to a new location every morning. I enjoyed the drives down the jungle lanes and through the pretty villages here. It's cooler here and there is no rain so I am much more comfortable.

As soon as we pull into a new site we set up our defense then we are free to do as we please. Each stopping place we get together, four or five guys, and walk into the countryside. We never go over a couple of miles from the perimeter. We've always been able to find a pineapple grove with a well under a stand of banana trees. We bathe, eat pineapples, and pick bananas. We are flown in drinking water only so these forays into the countryside are necessary. Yesterday we bought four chickens from a village we found and last night we roasted them. They were tough but we enjoyed the first hot meal we have had in nearly a month. It seems we are living off the land and what we can buy from the people more than what the Army gives us.

Saigon radio reported today that our unit had been withdrawn from Cambodia. I have news for them. We are farther in than ever and we don't plan to leave soon. Well that's all for now. I'll write again soon.

Love,
Ray

CHAPTER 5
BETWEEN NAM AND NAM

Lost

I HAD A great friend during my young and early adult life, Tom Hannsz. We always liked the thought of flying. We used to go to the private plane showrooms around Hobby Airport just to look and dream. About our second year at the U of H, 1966, we entered ground school at Hull Field in Sugar Land, which we completed and passed the test. Then we were assigned to our planes and instructors. After about seven or eight hours we both soloed. It took forty-five flying hours to get a private pilot license; a substantial amount was with an instructor, but the majority was practicing solo. We solo practiced together and tore up the skies around Houston. One day we were practicing touch-and-go landings at various airports: La Porte, Spaceland, and Scholes Field at Galveston (all uncontrolled). Tom was a good pilot and flew by the book. Me, not so much (maybe a little Pete Mitchell there). We were approaching Spaceland airport and the pattern was empty. Tom lined up to make a normal approach and initially enter the downwind leg. I realized I was in position to enter immediately on base and radioed Tom to tell him that's what I was going to do. In freeway-driving terms, it would be like recklessly cutting someone off to beat them to an exit ramp. So, I landed ahead of him, taxied to the office, parked, went in, and got a Coke. When Tom got down, and was in the office, he was pissed. Rightly. This wasn't the Gulf Freeway in your lane at 60 mph. It was a couple of planes flying at more than double that and no brakes. The only way Tom could have been angrier was if he found me sniffing around a couple of his girlfriends. Anyway, I hung my head in feigned shame and, after he let me suffer a minute or so, he forgave me. All back to normal. That was just the beginning of my flying experiences.

Got lost on my cross-country solo training trips a few times. On one cross-country, I flew to Austin and landed. Had a Coke, got back in my plane, and took off heading for Houston. Beautiful clear day. Was following my map. It's called pilotage and was heading for Luling as a checkpoint. When I got there and checked my map I knew I was lost. Luling didn't have a river around it. The town below me did, so it was not Luling. Tried to fly close enough to the water tower to read the town name but couldn't make it out. Saw a landing strip on the edge of this little town and decided to land to ask where I was. Was a little frustrated by this point and didn't pay attention to the wind sock. Tried twice to land with the wind on the short runway and had to go around both times. Finally figured out the problem, approached the runway against the wind, and landed. Taxied to the small office by the field. Parked my Cessna 150 and went into the office. The guys there asked me if I was the guy having a problem landing. I said, "Yes. Where am I?" They howled. Embarrassing, but they told me where I was: Sequin. I got back in my plane and headed to Sugar Land. Paid more attention and got back with no issues.

I eventually got my license and spent a lot of time flying around the Houston area. I was nineteen. Took my parents on a ride to Galveston in a Cessna 182 (had upgraded from a two-seater to a four-seater). Mom must have really trusted me because she fell asleep in the back seat. Took my brother, Ken Luce, and sister-in-law, Terri Luce, on a flight. Not sure why but decided to make a stop at Hobby. Busy airport. I asked flight control for a short approach and made a fairly radical landing. In flight training you learn to overcome your tendency to lean in a turn. Ken had no such training. As I banked into a steep descending turn, he was leaning hard on the front right seat door. Lots of fun. Then I got drafted.

After Vietnam, I was living in New Orleans and had some spare time. I had the GI Bill benefits, but already had my college degree. However, I learned that, if I had a private pilot license, the government would pay 90 percent of my commercial pilot training. Great deal. So, I entered the program. Ended up flying a Piper Arrow: four-seats, variable speed prop, retractable landing gear and pretty fast, about 160 miles an hour cruise speed. Loved flying that plane. Several of us used to fly a half-dozen planes or more to Destin, Florida, for a barbecue, a fly-in. No alcohol involved but a great beach party. On cool, clear nights, I used to love night flying north of lake Pontchartrain around Bogalusa. So clear. Could see so far. Practiced touch-and-goes at Bogalusa. Uncontrolled airport. Great runway lighting system. Tune radio to a certain frequency and key the mike. Magically, the airport landing lights came on. Took some friends with me on occasion. Flew New Orleans to Houston several times. Once, David Berryhill and his wife, Leslie, flew with me. When we landed at Lakefront Airport the touchdown was so gentle that it was almost imperceptible. I think Dave was impressed. Leslie needed to hit the john quick. I asked her why she didn't say something earlier. I could have landed at Lafayette for a break—no problem. Then the "Lost" happened.

It was the July 4, 1976 holiday, our nation's two hundredth anniversary. I had a doc friend, Pat Mullins. Crazy guy. He had a girlfriend in New Orleans but an old girlfriend in Connecticut. He invited the old girlfriend to visit. I was with Pat and his current girlfriend when number two showed up. It quickly became awkward, but I stepped in as the knight in shining armor and volunteered to rescue the stranded damsel in distress, which I did. I was flying the Arrow the next day to Houston for a Fourth of July party at my brother, Ken's, house and I invited her to go. So, the next day we got in the plane and flew to Houston no problem. Great party, but not much drinking for me. Had to fly back to New Orleans the next day. We spent the night at a friend's house and got up early the next morning to fly back to New Orleans from Hobby. Not good weather. Low ceiling. Low visibility, and I was a visual flight rules (VFR) pilot, not instrument flight rules (IFR) trained. Five minutes after I left Hobby, I was lost. Could see the ground but that's about it; almost IFR conditions, except I knew how to use my radio navigation systems. Couldn't get over eight hundred or nine hundred feet or would be in the overcast. Not good for a VFR pilot. Plus, I knew that east of Hobby there were some radio towers at that altitude. All in all, I was a little nervous, but had to remain calm, if for no other reason not to upset my passenger. Finally, I tuned in on the Beaumont omni navigational beacon, which is located on the airport property. The Arrow was fast and made it to Beaumont pretty quick. Could tell from my instruments that we were close, and still low, at eight hundred feet, which is a dangerous altitude around an airport. I passed over the Beaumont runways. Safe. Landed and went into the Flight Service Station. The weather guys told me it would be the same all the way to New Orleans. What to do?

I had a plan. We got back in the plane and I took off. I flew just a couple of minutes south and there was I-10. Followed I-10 all the way back to New Orleans, eight hundred to one thousand feet and staying to the right. I was hoping that if anyone was flying west and following I-10 they were staying to their right. Finally made it to New Orleans and followed the southern shore of Lake Pontchartrain all the way to Lakefront Airport and landed. Safe. But a great experience, lost or not.

The Orange Crush and a Lost Super Bowl Playbook

SUPER BOWL 1978 was a great matchup for me and my Braniff International colleagues. Braniff was headquartered in Dallas and provided the charter aircraft for the Dallas Cowboys for all their out of town games. Braniff even had a Cowboy helmet painted on the tail of the aircraft we used. Big deal then.

Not connected, Braniff flew an orange 747, the "Big Orange," round-trip every day from Dallas to Honolulu. As it turns out, the Denver Bronco team then was known as the "Orange Crush." So, they reached out to Braniff and chartered our orange 747 to fly them into New Orleans for the 1978 Super Bowl. Guess they thought it would be good publicity and it was. So, both Super Bowl teams, Cowboys and Broncos, flew to New Orleans on Braniff. I was a Braniff sales representative in New Orleans at the time. So, it was lots of work for me helping to plan the logistics of the arrival.

Both teams flew in the same day, the Cowboys first. No problems. Didn't use the terminal. Offloaded them on the tarmac directly from the airplane to the busses. Off to hotel. Gone. Done. Just waiting on the Broncos.

Basically, it was the same with the Broncos, just a little

later. Big Orange taxied to the bus pickup area and parked. We offloaded them onto the busses and sent them to their hotel. Then things went south.

Remember, this is before cell phones. After we sent the Broncos to their hotel, I was at the Braniff ticket counter in the terminal. One of the Bronco coaches approached me. Recognized me from the arrival. He was panicked. He told me one of the players left his Super Bowl playbook on the plane. Big problem for the Broncos and the player. Huge fine for the player. I immediately worked with my Braniff airport guys to get in touch with Big Orange. We did, and it was on taxi to take off. Explained what the issue was. Big Orange pulled to the side of taxiway while crew looked for the playbook. I jumped into a Braniff pickup truck with a mechanic and we drove out to Big Orange. We were in radio contact. The flight attendants found the playbook in a seatback pocket.

I didn't know this, but the pilots have a rope, better described as line, in the cockpit. The cockpit of a 747 is over twenty feet above surface. The mechanic and I pulled next to the nose of the plane and the captain opened his cockpit window. He carefully lowered the playbook to us in a bag tied to the line. Done. Had it in my hands. Back to the terminal.

So, there I was with the Denver Bronco Super Bowl playbook; I had to take it to the hotel. I sniffed something important. On a pay phone, I called one of my buddies, George Mcamman. Knew he was a gambler. Told him what I had; asked him what to do. He had no hesitation: "Find a copy machine." I didn't. I'm an Eagle Scout.

I drove to the Bronco's hotel with the playbook, parked, went in, and found the player's room. Could hear guys noisily partying inside. Knocked. "Who Dat?" Maybe where the famous Saint's saying came from. I said, "I'm Ray Luce with

Braniff. I have your playbook." Door immediately cracked. Distinctive smell emanated. Already partying. Invited me to come in, but I declined and just handed him the playbook. In retrospect, should have gone in. But lots of excitement in any case. By the way, Denver lost to Dallas.

Charity Hospital and a Roll of Toilet Paper

THE EVENING BEFORE Super Bowl 1978 was not the best for me. I attended a huge, official NFL Super Bowl party that evening near the New Orleans French Quarter and headed home late. Terrible weather. At a treacherous turn under the freeway, I lost control of my vehicle and plowed into a freeway pillar. Not good. Lots of pain. I remember being extracted from my van but nothing after until I was going to surgery in New Orleans Charity Hospital. Doc said, "We may not be able to save your leg." I said, "Just do the best you can." Woke up in a daze the next day in the Charity Hospital prison ward.

As it turns out, I was in the Charity Hospital orthopedic ward. Most gunshot and knife wounds result in orthopedic bone or sinew injuries; they are apparently common among violent offenders. Therefore, all orthopedic patients were placed in the prison ward. So, there I was.

Was a long room. Maybe four beds on the side opposite me by the double doors, two on the end wall below the clock, and six on my side; like a horseshoe of beds. Every patient was black, except me—all prisoners from the local New Orleans Parish Prison or the Louisiana State prison, Angola.

Don't remember for sure but the parish prisoners had blue bands on their arms and the state prisoners had red bands on their arms. Some were handcuffed to their beds. Civilians, like me, had white bands. There was one other guy with a white band, a New Orleans policeman I believe, but he left a day or two after I arrived. So, it was only me and almost a dozen black prisoners, all of us in a lot of pain.

I can't describe the pain I felt—trapped in my body and nowhere to go, but pain. My right leg was elevated in traction, my right arm was in a cast, and I had an IV in the back of my left hand. Most of the other guys were hurting the same. At the end of the room, up on the wall, was a clock. We got our morphine shots every three or four hours. All of us were watching the clock like addicts—not from a morphine addiction, just to ease the pain. Loved the relief from pain the morphine provided. But it was still the prison ward. We had an armed guard at the end of the room opposite the clock. He was on a raised platform and his job was to monitor the prisoners. Guards changed but we were guarded twenty-four hours a day. Amazing experience for your average young, white working guy.

Just a few days in, a young black guy (I was thirty-three and I'm guessing he was around twenty-three) came in with a gunshot wound that resulted in a shattered femur. Nice looking guy. Good shape. Talked to him some. Intelligent. But 100 percent focused on "When I get out of here, I'm going to kill that son of a bitch." Big education for me. Don't understand the (gang?) hate but it's there. And the days rolled by.

After a few days, I was in less pain and able to focus more. Noticed a couple of the other guys (prisoners) had girlfriends visiting them. Some of the girlfriends brought drugs (pills) to them. After the girlfriends left, the guys with the pills started doing "orthopedic wing" drug deals. They figured out their trade deals and, to do the deal, wrapped their pills in toilet paper and stuffed the wad into the center of the roll. Every prisoner (me included, although not a prisoner) had a personal roll of toilet paper. The plan was each guy would toss the rolls from bed to bed until the deal was done. Great, except I only had my left arm and hand working. I must interject here that every night the guard fell asleep and started snoring. That was the starting gun for the exchange. The first night there was a guy in the bed to my left, a prisoner from Louisiana's Angola prison. Interestingly, Angola prisoners handmade Billy Graham's simple casket.

The exchange started. Toilet paper rolls were tossed bed to bed. Even though I only had my left arm and hand working, and I'm right handed, I performed like a champion. Initially, the black prisoners were looking at me very skeptically. But I made enough good tosses to earn their trust. Then came the big toss. The Angola prisoner to my left was moved out. So, I had an empty bed between me and the next bed to my left. When the toss began that night, and the toilet paper roll came to me, I had to make a two-bed toss left handed. All the black prisoners were focused on me. "Don't screw up, honkey." I didn't. Left handed, over an empty bed, I made a perfect toss. Hit the guy in the hands, like the game-winning pass at the Super Bowl with ten seconds left on the clock. But he dropped the toss and the toilet paper roll landed on the floor and started unrolling. The guard was still asleep. Just then a brother from another ward came rolling in on his wheelchair. All the brothers were waving at him and pointing at the roll. He got the message and retrieved the roll, drugs inside.

The upshot of this story is that the black prisoners knew

that I made a perfect, two-bed toss and the brother screwed up. A few days later I was transferred to Tulane hospital and spent three months there in traction. That's a long time on your back in a hospital. Lots of stories from that experience.

It's a Bitch to Lose a Presidential Election

WHEN I WAS 11 years old, in 1957, Ike Eisenhower was president, and I was under the impression that our president was some kind of deity. At the time, that was understandable. It was only twelve years after WWII ended and Ike was instrumental in that incredible victory. The American people revered him. I don't remember his predecessor, Truman, but I remember Ike. Including Truman and Ike, I've lived during the administrations of thirteen presidents. In 1957, it was inconceivable to me that I would ever see a president in person. But I eventually saw and/or interacted with five. This is that story.

President John Kennedy: During November 1963, President Kennedy visited Houston. As planned he landed at Hobby and his motorcade moved down Broadway to the Gulf Freeway on the way to the Rice Hotel. My best friend, Tom Hannsz, and I parked Tom's car on the Broadway curb and were standing on the hood when JFK came by. We were less than ten feet from Kennedy's open limousine as it passed and, moving slowly, he looked us both in the eye for a brief second. Kennedy was assassinated the next day in Dallas.

President George H. W. Bush (HW): My interaction with

HW is the crux of the story and I will fully describe below. Please bear with me until I get there.

President Lyndon Johnson: During 1968, President Johnson visited the Manned Spacecraft Center where I was working in the Public Affairs Office. He toured our museum and my boss, my boss's boss, and I were just inside the museum doors to welcome the president. As he entered, he shook our hands one by one. I can tell you that Johnson had a strong grip. As he left us and headed to a Gemini capsule for a briefing, I tried to follow, but I instantly had a Secret Service officer in front of me with his hand on my chest. But a pretty close encounter.

Bill Clinton: I don't remember the exact year, but it was during his second term. My Continental Airlines boss, Dave Hilfman, was on the advisory board of a national education group. They were meeting in Los Angeles and Dave couldn't make the meeting. I was his corporate attorney and the group's bylaws permitted a board member to send an alternate. Dave sent me. During one of the lunches I was seated at the advisory board's table right in front of the stage. Among others, Clinton was a speaker. He was maybe twenty feet away. Don't remember what he said, but I do remember that the lady next to me was swooning over him—maybe ready to pull a "Monica." Interesting lunch.

President George W. Bush (W): Easter of 2001 or 2002, while I was working for Continental Airlines in the Sales Department, Continental was the airline sponsor of the annual White House Easter Egg Roll. I attended with some customers, had breakfast in the White House and, shortly after, W appeared and spoke for a few minutes. Very intimate meeting.

Back to HW: During the fall of 1964, Goldwater was locked in a heated presidential election with Johnson. I had just entered the University of Houston. Goldwater visited Houston and spoke at the "temporary" Colt 45 baseball field next to the under-construction Astrodome. I attended. It was my first political event. Before Goldwater spoke, a young guy named George H. W. Bush spoke. He was running for Congress for the first time. He lost that election. But that was my first encounter with HW.

HW was eventually elected to Congress in 1966. At the time, I was working at the Manned Spacecraft Center in the public affairs office. One day I was walking through the lobby of our offices when this tall guy in a light blue blazer walked in the door. He looked a little lost and I recognized him. He was HW. I stopped and asked if I could help him. He told me who he was looking for (one of our public affairs bosses), and I escorted him to that office.

During 1986, while HW was VP, Continental Airlines sponsored the Doug Sanders Celebrity Golf Tournament in Houston; there were lots of topline celebrities. Continental sponsored a VIP hospitality tent and HW spent some time there with us. I was in charge of the tent, so had the opportunity to visit with him.

The last time I saw HW in person was early 1989; Clinton won the 1988 election, and HW was out of office January 1989. I was on a Continental Airlines business trip to Washington DC. After a couple of days, I was catching a 2 p.m. nonstop flight from Washington National back to Houston Intercontinental. When my boarding row was called, I was headed to 10D, an aisle coach seat. I walked through first class into coach and in 8C (aisle coach) there sat HW. It had only been a month or two since Clinton was sworn in and I was tempted to comment: "It's a bitch to lose an election." But my mom raised me with better manners. I kept my mouth shut and took my seat two rows back on the opposite side of the aisle. I was trying to figure out what the president of the United States was doing in coach?

The flight was full, but before the cabin door shut, a Continental flight attendant came and got HW and moved him up front—but not the 2 guys in row 8D and E, the aisle across from 8C. I had noticed these guys earlier, had seen the type at the Manned Spacecraft Center. All business. Dark suites. Dark ties. Secret Service buttons on their lapels. Anyway, the boarding door was shut, we pushed off the gate, taxied to the runway, and left for Houston.

During the flight I was visiting the cabin crew in the rear galley and asked them what the president of the United States was doing in coach. They told me that he booked at the last minute and there were no more first-class seats. In our (thankfully and hopefully for always) egalitarian country, you don't throw a regular citizen out of first-class just to reseat a VIP. So, I asked what happened. The crew told me that they announced to the first-class passengers that the president of the United States was seated in coach and asked whether anyone would be willing to give up their seat in first for him. It was a unanimous decision—probably a lot of Republicans flying from DC back to Houston. So HW was moved up to first. At least the guy that gave up his first-class seat had a great story to tell.

But the flight was not quite over. When we landed in Houston, everyone was requested to remain seated. HW was taken down the jetway stairs, just outside the aircraft door, to a waiting limousine. The two muscle men in 8D and E got up and took their bags out of the overhead. Very heavy and bulky. I'm thinking heavy, heavy ordinance. I was probably pretty safe on that flight.

The Death of a Salesman Postponed

WAS IN THE nineties. Worked in the Continental Airlines sales office in Houston at the headquarters. I was a National Sales Manager. Handled top travel management customers. Cush job. Lots of recognition and envy being in that position. So, had to be 100 percent effective daily or risk being replaced. Corporate America. Like playing in the Super Bowl every day. Was able to participate in some really nice customer events. One of the best was flying to Seattle to accept the "keys" from Boeing for Continental's delivery of its first 777.

Met my customer, Ron Blaylock, President of International Tours, in Seattle. Settled into hotel. Nice place. First-class. All attendees assembling there. Maybe close to two hundred. First evening was a cocktail party in the lobby, followed by buses to a wonderful restaurant. The participants were impressive: Continental executive-suite officers, sales and marketing VPs and directors, corporate communications (public affairs) VPs and directors, all my bosses, key customers, and the travel industry press. High-powered group. One cocktail over the line and your career was finished. Lots on the line.

Bought a special outfit for this deal: black shoes, black

slacks, black belt, double-breasted houndstooth jacket, and carefully selected matching tie. Was heading for the kick-off cocktail party. Hotel elevators opened onto the lobby. At lobby level, elevators landed on a raised area two or three steps above and overlooking the lobby level. When the doors opened and you stepped out, you were very visible—almost like a presentation. Got in the elevator. Pushed lobby button. A few floors down the elevator stopped and the doors opened. I walked off. Heart stopped. A room full of all the people my career depended on and, to a man (gals were all dressed elegantly too), all were wearing dark grey or navy-blue suits with red ties. I'm done. Career done. All night standing out as a nonconformist creep. Deepest crevasse I've ever been in. Then, while I was standing there, melting down, another elevator arrived and Continental's Chief Executive Officer, Gordon Bethune, stepped off. Life vest. Lifeboat. Instant resurrection. Gordon was wearing black shoes, black slacks, a black belt, a houndstooth jacket, and a carefully selected matching tie. Heart began to beat again.

During the evening, I never attempted to talk to Gordon. The constant parade of folks that wanted to talk to him were way above my pay grade. But I spent all evening close enough to Gordon for everyone to know that I was on the cutting edge of Continental corporate fashion. Saved.

The next day, the Continental folks and all our guests went to the Boeing plant, got our "keys" to the new 777, and flew back to Houston. First-class service throughout. Great plane. Great trip. Water cannons to taxi through when we arrived in Houston.

The Last High Country Shootout and a Signed Eagles Guitar

THE BEST JOB I ever had was working for Continental Airlines in National Sales as a national sales manager. Over time, I managed several national travel-agency accounts, but my favorite was International Tours. Continental knew how to entertain its top distributors and that resulted in having some great times with International Tours and especially with their president, Ron Blaylock. We managed to participate in some fabulous events. Ron and I made it to The People's Choice Awards a couple of times and the Grammy Awards once—fun events to the tenth power. Were held in Los Angeles. Always stayed at the Beverly Hilton Hotel. In 1993 a limo took us on a tuxedo ride from the Hilton to the Shrine Auditorium for the thirty-fifth Grammys. Great early afternoon ride. Beautiful California weather. Sunroof open on the limo. Ron and I were shooting champagne corks twenty feet into the air thorough the sunroof driving down Wilshire Boulevard, like a nuclear sub firing ballistic missiles from below surface. Loved that Grammys event. The opening was a wild song and dance routine by Madonna and there was a great duet, Celine Dion and Peabo Bryson, singing "Beauty and the Beast." The Grammys after-party was spectacular. What fun times!

Another annual event I participated in with Ron and International Tours was the Mickey Mantle Make-a-Wish Foundation Celebrity Golf Classic held at Shangrl-La Resort on Grand Lake in northeast Oklahoma. Mickey was an Oklahoma native. The golf tournament was off the charts. All the great Yankees that played with Mickey were there, plus other celebrities. One year, Ron and I played with Yogi Berra in our foursome. Yogi was constantly coaching me. On one hole, he told me to hit the ball straight down the center of the fairway, which I did. But Yogi complained that I didn't hit it far enough. I said, "But Coach, you didn't tell me how far to hit it." Another year both Roy Clark and Toby Keith played in our foursome. The night before, Roy and Toby jammed together, until the wee hours, at that night's dinner party. Roy didn't make our tee time. Joined us maybe on the third hole. Was a scramble and we were playing best ball. Once on the third-hole green, we were looking at a thirty-foot put. Through bloodshot eyes, Roy drained it. On the "Mickey Hole," a par 3, as foursomes cycled through, Mantle hit a ball from the tee box to the green. For a foursome donation to the Make-a-Wish Foundation, could play from Mickey's green shot. He was invariably close to the hole. All in all, just a lot of fun and great memories. But the best was the High Country Shootout.

If there seems to be a sports theme running through this vignette, it's because Ron was a star college athlete and coach. His major claim to fame was that, as the Kansas State quarterback in 1959 (jersey number 14) in Manhattan, Kansas, he led the Kansas State Wildcats to a 29-14 victory over the University of Nebraska. Unheard of. Nebraska never loses to the Wildcats in Manhattan. Ron broke that tradition and it didn't happen again for forty years. But back to the High Country Shootout.

Ed Podolak played for the Kansas City Chiefs as a star running back for nine seasons (1969-1977), including a Super Bowl championship in 1970. Great guy and a good friend of Ron. Podolak ended up living in Aspen, Colorado. During the late eighties, Podolak hooked-up with Jimmy Buffet and they started the High Country Shootout as an annual charity event in Aspen. Ron was involved from the beginning. After a few years, Buffet left the event and Podolak replaced him with the Eagles. In the early nineties, for about four years, I was there. As a sponsor, Continental provided free tickets to fly in the celebrities and, with International Tours and Ron, I had a ringside seat.

The Hotel Jerome was the High Country Shootout headquarters. The sequence of events was: day-one arrivals and big party that night, day-two golf tournament and private Eagles concert that evening, and day-three relax with a going away party that night. There were tons of sports celebrities. Don't know Podolak's Raiders connection but many Oakland Raiders stars were always there. Of course, because of his Chiefs connection, many Chiefs stars were there as well. As it turns out, Kevin Costner had a place in Aspen during those years and he always attended, but not just for a cameo. He played in our golf tournament and attended the private Eagles concert. All in all, there were a lot of high rollers, many flying in on private jets and planning to spend some big bucks.

The second night's party, the private Eagles concert, was spectacular. Don't remember the name but the bar held about two hundred folks. Was two level. There was a lower level where the band played with a dance floor surrounded by restaurant-type booths. Just above and tapered back like a bowl was the upper level with tables and a couple of bars. The upper level folks had a full view of the lower level. Before the Eagles performed, Glenn Frey would auction off just a few items, mostly Raiders or Chiefs signed memorabilia, but they were rare. My impression was the movers and shakers kind of know which high rollers were going to bid and they did. A football signed by all the Chiefs would go for $20,000 or $30,000. Basically, it was all for charity and bragging rights among millionaires. Was impressive. The last night's party was great as well. Podolak always auctioned off a guitar signed by all the Eagles. During the years I attended, the price for the guitar kept declining: $40,000, $20,000, $10,000—you can see where this is heading. Following, in sequence, are some of my memories of the events.

The High Country Shootout golf tournament was the best I ever participated in. Podolak arranged it so that on every hole one of the Aspen hotels or restaurants had a tent with a bar and great food. How much can you eat and drink? Apparently, a lot. The celebrities were awesome. I remember one of the Raiders taking a Raiders "Death Stick" driver out of the plastic packaging, ready to hit some golf balls. One year, everyone was having such a good time partying the night before that we didn't put our foursome parings together. The next morning at the course, total confusion. Podolak got on a microphone and announced, "We are on the cutting edge of Golf. Get on a cart and go play golf." That's what we did and was a great day.

One of the evenings at the Eagles concert, I remember that Kevin Costner was sitting in a booth on the lower level. I was with my friends on the upper level. We noticed that there was a line of at least a dozen beautiful young women queuing up to meet Costner. Have no idea what they said or what he said, but I was envious. Don't remember any cute girls lining up to talk to me. But it got better. Later, I was with one of my Continental friends, Jim Gallo, on the upper level. I was standing to Gallo's right. Suddenly, Gallo noticed all the girls in the club were looking at him. I believe it made him nervous. He mentioned it to me. Then he looked to his left. Kevin Costner was standing next to him. Jim said to Kevin, "Oh, I thought they were looking at me." Kevin said, "They were." Costner was just a good guy. The private Eagles concert was so fabulous.

As the years rolled by, there were fewer and fewer private jets parked at the Aspen airport, and the eye-popping amounts paid for the sports memorabilia and the signed Eagles guitar kept dropping. But we are creatures of habit and, somehow, don't recognize change—like the frog in a slowly warming pot of water over a low flame. That's about where we were at the last High Country Shootout I ever attended. The last night's going away dinner at the Hotel Jerome was always special. Barbecue was cooked outside all day. Bars were open. Everyone lubed up pretty good, including Ron and me. As the evening progressed, it was time to auction the signed Eagles guitar. Should have gone for $10,000 at least. Podolak went to the podium and became the auction master. Having been at so many Shootouts and knowing the history, Ron decided to open the bidding. He bid $5,000. At first, Ron was smug. Got some "street cred" for bidding such an auspicious amount. Podolak was asking for more: "Can I get $10,000? Can I. . . Can I . . . Can I?" No takers. Saw Ron start to turn pale. Was before cell phones. Saw what was going to happen. Was feeling in my pocket for a quarter in case I had to go to a pay phone and call an ambulance. "Going once." "Going twice." "Sold to Ron Blaylock for $5,000." The best I could do to console Ron was turn to him and say, "Ron, if it's down to the point where we are the 'high rollers,' this deal is over." True. That was the last High Country Shootout.

Almost a quarter of a century later, Ron and I are still working on a marketing plan to sell that signed Eagles guitar and recoup his money. But frankly, between the experience and the story—plus it was for charity—it was worth the money.

A Buffalo Burger Bash

THIS IS ESSENTIALLY a comment on the changing of the guard in our nation and the east end of Houston in particular. The following is as originally written in March, 2014.

On March 8, 2014, the Milby High School Alumni Association held a "Burger Bash" at the old campus and I attended. Fabulous. I had not walked through those doors since I walked out the last time fifty years before. There's a great vibe there. I was astonished by the character and quality of the students. They hosted, I'm guessing, between one hundred fifty and two hundred alumni and they were the most poised and polite young folks you could ever meet. The entire drive is focused on learning, achievement, and success. The demographics are much different than in our day. But if you've been in the east end of Houston recently, you know things are changing there. I recently drove from Minute Maid Park down Texas Avenue/Harrisburg/Broadway to Milby, Deady, and the Park Place Boulevard/Broadway circle. A streetcar line is opening along that route from downtown Houston to near the ship channel turning basin. A renaissance is taking place in our backyard, and I'm positive about where it's heading because Milby sits there in the center like an impervious rock.

The alums attending were from all eras. A family brought

a very elderly Milby WWII veteran wearing his identifying headgear. Very special. Very rare. Another alum was class of '46, the year I was born. Tours were offered every thirty minutes. One of the classrooms near the entrance has been turned into a Milby museum. The old auditorium is the library. After the tour they let us sign a set of alumni lockers with a Marks-A-Lot. If our old principal, Roscoe Bayless, caught one of us doing that back in the day, justice would have been sure and swift: *A Green Mile* walk with a discipline note to the gym and coach Truelove—five pops minimum. A life-size buffalo has been installed at the entrance of the school where we used to wait for the bell to ring so we could head to home room. Also, a tribute to the great 1961 football team, the year I entered, has been installed on the front lawn. If you were there, you remember the excitement and their names. The dream died only one game from playing for the Texas state championship. David Roessler from the team was there and it was great to talk to him. (Unfortunately, our dear classmate, David, died December 31, 2017.)

There was some solemn time. The Alumni Association has installed a large polished granite plaque near the front entrance. The names of Milby students killed in combat during WWII, Korea, Vietnam, Somalia, and Iraq are engraved there. Among the twenty-one killed in Vietnam, there are three of my contemporary classmate's names: Richard Honey, Davis Butcher, and Bob McIntyre. Bob and I were together beginning with kindergarten at Park Place Elementary. The sad thing is that there is room for more names on the plaque. Pray the space remains blank. Say a prayer for peace.

Chapter 6
Vietnam and Cambodia Redux

Note: Following is the journal I, Ray W. Luce, kept during my 2016 return to Vietnam and Cambodia. It is provided here essentially as written. For example, where written in the present tense, the present tense is maintained.

Singapore Airlines Club, Singapore

Journal Entry, March 19, 2016

Been flying for over 24 hours and sitting in the Singapore Airlines Club in Singapore. My 2-hour flight to Saigon leaves in about 3 hours. After 46 years, like my WWII predecessors, I'm returning to my old battlefields, in Vietnam and Cambodia. Will be in country about 2 weeks; much less than the 14 months I spent there so long ago. Thoughts from my 1970 trip over follow:

25FEB70, Wednesday

My flight, from Houston to San Francisco, marked the last experience I would have of the "World," American 20th century civilization, before being inserted into the technikill conflict of Vietnam. They paged us to U.S. military assembly areas in the San Francisco Airport, collected our orders and moved us onto buses for transfer to Oakland Army Terminal. The process had begun; endless paperwork to complete, and fleeting friendships to make.

I had only had my dress greens a few weeks, and now I was trading them in for jungle fatigues, jungle boots, flak jacket and helmet. At Oakland, they issued us everything we would need, except our weapons and our courage. And the system was efficient. I only slept one night in the bunk assigned to me.

26FEB70, Thursday

We spent most of the afternoon in a Travis A.F.B. hangar, waiting for our transport to the "Republic," Republic of Vietnam. The hangar was cavernous. On the other side, returning troops were made to strip and deposit their jungle issue into huge wooden bins. They were too far away to see the look in their eyes, but the contrast between our new clothes and the rags they wore was a clear signal of things to come. We boarded our transport late in the evening. Courtesy of the Military Airlift Command we rode over on Overseas National Airlines, one of many carriers assembled to operate the 10,000-mile-long pressurized, aluminum troop-pipeline.

The plane was an all coach configuration 707. The hostesses had been on this run for a while. And they looked at us with a kind of sadness. After all, they were our contemporaries, and had made the ride "back" with our returning counterparts. They were a rare group of American civilians. They saw the war first hand; even if only on the fringes. We took off late in the evening, and left the land of the free and the home of the brave behind. I had made friends during processing and we talked. It was a long ride to Vietnam.

GOD SAID LET THERE BE LIGHT AND THERE WAS "LLUMO"

27FEB70, Friday

The total transit time was over 24 hours. We stopped in Honolulu and Okinawa for fuel. About an hour out we were on our descent into Honolulu.

They let us roam around in the main Honolulu passenger terminal while the plane was refueled. There were a lot of American tourists there, and we felt pretty conspicuous in our jungle combat dress. More civilians exposed to the fringes of the war. Anyway, I was excited. Never been there before. I went up to a souvenir counter and picked out some post cards from a rack. I wrote some short notes, addressed them, bought stamps from a machine, and mailed them. It never occurred to me to pay for the cards. With a new load of fuel, we left Honolulu and continued to Okinawa. It was a long leg. They let us off the plane in Okinawa, so we could stretch our legs. Then, back in the plane for the final leg into Vietnam.

Saigon Arrival

Journal Entry, March 20, 2016

I landed at Ho Chi Minh City's Tan Son Nhut airport yesterday, Saturday. Been there before. Much different; just a few remnants from what the Vietnamese call the "American War"; mostly large concrete enclosures built to protect parked U.S. fighter aircraft. Probably too much trouble to demolish. The terminal is new and modern, plus air-conditioned. What a break. I didn't check any luggage, moved through immigration and customs quickly and walked out of the terminal. There were lots of greeters with signs waiting. I saw the sign I was looking for and a couple of nice young guys loaded me into an air-conditioned car for the ride to my hotel. Beautiful hotel and great staff, the Park Hyatt Saigon. I had been in in transit almost 36 hours, up longer, and was dead tired; too tired to explore, even though it was early in the day. So, I just went to a Circle K (they are all over the city) across the street from the Hyatt, bought a cold Heineken to take to my room, took a shower, closed the blackout shutters in my room, drank the Heineken and went to sleep.

My wakeup call was 6:00 a.m. this morning, Sunday. I spent a couple of hours at the Hyatt's beautiful breakfast buffet studying Maps of Ho Chi Minh City and planning my day. By 9:00a.m. I was on the street dodging motor bikes, thousands of them. Better than dodging bullets I guess but maybe just as dangerous for "out of towners." The streets are a zoo and I was afraid to cross a few of them. Planning where and how to cross is like solving a Rubik's Cube.

Overall, Saigon has been transformed. It's a modern, bustling Asian metropolis; no more concertina wire, sandbagged buildings or troops. And the vibe is great. The population is young, friendly and happy, at least they certainly seem to be. The streets are clean. There are tons of hotels, restaurants and bars, and lots to see. My pedometer claims I walked about 6 miles before I took a break for lunch and went to the hotel for some down time.

On my walk, I visited the Saigon zoo, which I remembered from my first visit. Many families were there and groups of young folks. Like Central Park in New York, it's an expansive green space in the middle of a concrete jungle; very lively and colorful. Enjoyed it. Saw lots of stately, French colonial architecture. The buildings were here in 1970 but have been mostly restored to their former glory. I spotted some kind of outdoor war museum and had to check that out. The displays included a surface to air missile (SAM) launcher. SAMs took down a lot of our planes over North Vietnam. Plans for this evening are to join the other members of the cruise up the Mekong for dinner at a French villa. Great day and the weather is good, although pretty warm. Going to Cu Chi tunnels tomorrow. They are near the Cambodian border. I spent a week there before my unit went to Cambodia and a week after my unit was withdrawn from Cambodia. Looking forward to it.

28FEB70, Saturday

As we began our final descent into Bien Hoa A.F.B. it became tense on the airplane. What had been a foreboding, mythical image was about to become very real. The plane landed and taxied to a stop. We deplaned onto the tarmac. They moved us a few hundred yards to a hangar for processing into country. The activity was incredible. Scores of helicopters beat their way across the sky, fighter-bombers were being serviced and armed, and there were a lot of troops in transit. Indelible images were flowing into me. Each hit with various degrees of incomprehension; truth and understanding were to come.

Who can forget one's first encounter with a real-in-life combat-hardened soldier? I was standing in the processing line, outside the hangar, when he walked by and then stopped a few feet away. He was black, over six feet tall and probably weighed about 200 pounds. It was difficult to tell because he carried so much gear. He was dressed like me; olive drab jungle fatigues, jungle boots and jungle sun hat. But the sameness ended there. His fatigues were incredibly worn and grimy. The leather sections of his boots weren't black like mine, but worn down to a natural leather buff color. He wore a huge backpack and a web belt with two canteens. His M16 hung loosely from his shoulder and he wore two or three bandoleers of ammunition. The Army had trained us to kill; this guy must have been at the top of his class. I thought "My God; is that what this place will create of me." I summoned the courage to speak to him; "Are you on your way home?" He looked at me in my new clothes and, like the old pro responding to a rookie's stupid question, answered "Naw man! I'm looking for transport to my fucking base camp." And he walked away.

The next image was one of the sadder realities of Vietnam. A hospital bus pulled up about 50 yards away, near an army transport plane. Medics began to unload wounded soldiers on stretchers onto the tarmac. There was no doubt these poor bastards were badly wounded. Most were hooked up to IV bottles. The bus left and the medics began loading the stretchers up the back loading-ramp into the transport. They loaded about a dozen of these poor guys. They were probably being flown to a military hospital in Japan, a medical way station for the seriously wounded on their way to VA hospitals in the World. And the reality of this place took a tighter hold. I asked myself; "would I be on a stretcher one day?" I was afraid to think about the more troublesome question. The line moved into the hangar and we were seated to fill out forms.

I can't remember all the irrelevant information we were asked to provide, but I do remember one particular question, "Are you in possession of any subversive literature?" I had already passed along my copy of *Che Guevara's Diary* and Martin Luther King's biography. But I had been reading, and had with me, a copy of Henry David Thoreau's *Civil Disobedience*. I checked the box "yes." The system was efficient, and a few hours after we turned our forms in I was located and led to a lieutenant. He asked to see the subversive literature I had claimed. When I handed him the classic work of this famous American transcendentalist, he looked at me like I was crazy. But Thoreau's message rang no less true. He shook his head and dismissed me.

We were finally loaded on buses and drove off the Bien Hoa base. It was about a nine-mile drive to Long Ben, one of the largest U.S. Army bases in Vietnam. Those miles afforded the first glimpses of the real Vietnam.

The bus was standard U.S. school bus issue, except for the olive drab color. It wasn't air conditioned (in the hottest country in the world) and there was wire mesh welded to the outside of the windows, which were open. I heard a guy ask his seatmate, "I wonder what the mesh covering the windows is for." But I knew; so none of the hundreds of Vietnamese we were passing could toss a grenade into the bus. And reality pressed upon me a little tighter. I asked myself a question, a question I asked many times, and maybe never got an answer, maybe never will: "Where am I?"

We arrived at Long Ben and were assigned to the 90th Replacement Battalion. They assigned us to barracks and bunks and we finally got a night's sleep.

Cu Chi Tunnels

Journal Entry, March 22, 2016

I'm not Captain Willard motoring up a river in Vietnam to terminate Colonel Kurtz's command (with extreme prejudice) but I am on a boat on the Mekong River setting off for Cambodia. And my mind is racing at 1,000 RPM. So, here's my report.

First, I must update you on the motorbike situation in Saigon. When I first reported, it was the weekend. Now it's the workweek, and the motorbike situation is to the 10th power worse. The motorbikes are like a river. The weekend was sort of Brazos or San Jacinto scale. Now think Amazonian. The rules are: walk across the street slowly but steadily, don't stop and don't move backward. As one of my guides said, "Think of the bikes as a river. Follow the rules and the waters will flow around you as if you're a stone in the stream." Pretty Zen stuff but, if you want to cross a street in Saigon, I can't think of a better philosophy. Now for the serious stuff. Yesterday I spent the morning at the Cu Chi tunnels 50+ miles out of Saigon and the afternoon at the War Remnants Museum in Saigon.

Cu Chi is a large region northwest of Saigon. It's at the end of the Ho Chi Minh Trail and is the gateway to Saigon. During the war, we considered it very important to defend. Google it for more information but know that over around 9 years VC fighters built about 150 miles of tunnels and thousands of the fighters and, in some cases their families, lived underground to hide while fighting the Americans (Stockholm syndrome setting in. Starting to sound like the briefers I've been listening to). Some of the heaviest fighting of the war was in that area. I spent a week there before my unit went to Cambodia and a week after my unit was withdrawn from Cambodia. I took the tour because I wanted to get out in the areas I had been in. I figured the Cu Chi tunnels would be some kind of Disney "Commie Land." Not close. It was a gut punch.

Today's tunnels are not a re-creation; just some restoration (i.e., the real deal). To begin, the guide took us to a VC era hooch; a 30' by 50', dirt-floor, thatch-roofed structure dug about 6' down in the ground so that the roof has a very low profile. There were benches and, in front, essentially an altar: North Vietnamese (all Vietnam now) red-with-yellow-star flag and a portrait of Ho Chi Minh. Plus, a large map of the Cu Chi area on one side of a TV in the center and a diorama of the Cu Chi tunnels (like an ant farm) on the other. It was hot and oppressive, and I began to feel a profound pressure. The briefer began his presentation and I realized it was essentially a propaganda pitch. Looking up at the portrait of Ho Chi Minh and the communist flag, I realized I was undergoing "reeducation." It was profoundly unsettling. Very uncomfortable. The presentation was civilized but America took a pretty bad rap. I'm a lawyer and I'm trained to look at issues from both (and other) points of view. The briefer didn't misrepresent the facts. He just had an

155

alternative interpretation of them. After the briefing, he showed us a black and white, sort of grainy, 1967 propaganda movie made in Hanoi during the war. All in all, one of the most intense moments of my life. While I was trying to breath, what I thought was real became so surreal that I couldn't tell the difference. The only analogies I can think of, and I don't think they are exact, would be a Confederate veteran visiting Gettysburg years after the battle or an older Japanese soldier visiting the Arizona memorial. The rest of the tour was gripping but not as intense: booby trap examples of how GIs were killed and maimed, life in the tunnels and etc. Extraordinary experience.

In the afternoon, I visited the War Remnants Museum in Saigon. It's essentially a very large, outdoor courtyard full of our finest weapons systems that were abandoned at the fall of Saigon in 1975, and 3 floors of very sophisticated and convincing propaganda that America was wrong in prosecuting the war, which could be (think Iraq). But the approach was different than Cu Chi. It was a powerful and more sophisticated psychological assault.

To sum from what I've learned from speaking with a quite a few Vietnamese, and aside from the communication barriers, the communists run Vietnam and there are a lot of them. And they harbor a lot of angst against the U.S. But there seems to be a lot of non-communists as well. The other thing is that the "American War" still consumes the society. Ho Chi Minh is their George Washington and the power of the state is omnipresent. But it's a young country demographically and I bet it progresses geometrically. If it ends up a stable, prosperous and U.S. friendly state, and I'm betting it does, maybe we won the war after all.

01MAR70, Sunday

The 90th Replacement Battalion was just a group of wooden barracks, with some sandbag protection, and interconnecting sandbagged walkways. Next to the barracks was a foot-ball-field-size assembly area. At one end of this area about a dozen telephone poles were erected; each with the name of a different Army installation stenciled on a sign nailed to the top of the pole. The sign could be seen from just about anywhere in the area. Every four hours, all day long, they assembled us (about 400 troops) and called out the names of the places on the poles, one by one, followed by the names of the troops who were assigned to that particular place. If your name was called, you were supposed to line up behind the proper pole. My name wasn't called today.

There was one humorous event though. About noon, on the way back to the barracks from one of these roulette sessions, a siren began to wail. All the new troops, me included, dove for cover behind the sandbags along the walkways. All the non-neophytes just laughed. We thought some kind of attack was going on; they just blew the siren every day at noon. I spent my second night at the 90th Replacement battalion.

02MAR70, Monday

My name was called at the first assembly. "Tan An . . . Luce." About a dozen of us were called for Tan An. A sergeant was waiting at the base of the Tan An pole and, as we lined up, he checked off our names. He loaded us into a deuce-and-a-half (2½ ton) truck and we were driven back to Bien Hoa. We unloaded next to a Caribou, a high-wing two-engine transport plane with a rear-loading ramp. We carried our gear, essentially just duffel bags, up the ramp and into the plane. We strapped into web sling seats. The ramp, which was hydraulic, was raised. We taxied to the runway and took off. Everything seemed to be happening pretty fast. It was only 50 miles to Tan An (officially designated Tan An Airstrip) and the flight only took 20 or 30 minutes. From the air, Tan An didn't look like much and it wasn't. It was just a fortified airstrip, which served as the 9th Infantry Division's headquarters. We landed, off loaded and, as soon as we were organized into a couple of columns, marched to the Go Devil Academy.

The Go Devil Academy was nothing more than a couple of two story wooden barracks, an administration building, and a couple of classrooms. All incoming 9th Infantry Division troops went through the academy. We were indoctrinated regarding what to expect in Vietnam. Also, we were trained in areas they never got into in stateside training (e.g., special weapons, demolitions, booby-traps, and etc.). I spent a week at the Academy before being assigned to my unit.

By the time we were processed into the Academy, and assigned a bunk, it was late in the afternoon. I was assigned guard duty, and after dinner reported to the officer of the guard. There were about 40 of us assigned to perimeter defense. We drew weapons, M16s (I hadn't been issued my personal weapon yet, and had to draw a weapon from the armorer every night for guard duty), and were assigned guard times and posts. We were dismissed, until it was our assigned time to stand guard.

We began to meet each other in the barracks. I listened to a lot of rumors; "last night a guy on guard lit a cigarette and a sniper put a round right through his head." I went to sleep. At about 2:00AM the officer of the guard woke me up; it was time for my shift.

I was assigned to walk a strip along the barbed wire about 50 to 75 yards long. It was dark and for the first time in country I was alone with my thoughts. I was dressed in jungle fatigues, flak jacket, and helmet. I had an M16 and a bandoleer of magazines. My shift lasted 4 hours, until about dawn. All night there was gunfire in the distance and in every direction. Over the jungle, several miles away, illumination flares (Ilumo) stayed in the air until it was daylight. I have never been as vigilant as I was that night, staring into the darkness, beyond the wire, looking for the enemy.

Long An Province

Journal Entry, March 23, 2016

Been cruising up the Mekong, including overnight, and the pace of my trip is more relaxed; a chance to exhale. Needed that. Left Saigon yesterday headed for My Tho, a decent sized city on the river where I caught my transportation to Cambodia. The trip from Saigon to My Tho took me within maybe 5 miles of my original base camp, Binh Phuoc, located about 10 miles south of Tan An, which I mentioned earlier. My main observation, similar to my Cu Chi experience, is that everything is so built up after 46 years.

In 1970, Saigon faded away quickly, and you were in the rural countryside. Not so today. A bypass, toll road has been built to connect Saigon with My Tho. And the build-up has followed the toll road. It's like Houston to Galveston; in 1970 there were lots of miles of empty country. Now it's city all the way. Same Saigon to My Tho. Anyway, I could see the rice paddies and I know that, not too far from the road, they are as expansive as ever. I flew over them when I arrived. But the real, noticeable difference is there are no water buffalos. During my whole trip, I haven't seen one. They used to be ubiquitous. Maybe they are still out in the countryside or maybe automation put them out of business. In any case, out in the boonies, Vietnam is still a village-oriented, rice-growing society. It is so sad that the war was raging around them while all they wanted to do was grow their rice, love their family and worship their ancestors. I've heard this sentiment several times from various guides on this trip. And I felt it when I was there during the war. One indicator is that, in 1970, I noticed that every family had a formal, above-ground graveyard by their house, so they could pay respect to mom, dad and earlier ancestors. Many were destroyed or left in disrepair due to the war. But they are back. The rice fields I could see are well tended and, in every case, the graveyards have been restored to their prominence and perfect repair. Ancestor worship is really a big deal here.

On the way to My Tho, a few miles out of Saigon, our guide told us we were entering Long An province. Rang big bells for me. Long An is a large area and that's what my Army unit was responsible for. I spent almost 3 months there, at Binh Phuoc, before my unit, 2nd Battalion (mechanized) 47th Infantry Regiment, left Binh Phuoc forever to move to the Cambodian border. Anyway, I became very familiar with the areas of Long An around Binh Phuoc. That's where I made a connection with the Vietnamese people. Maybe it's because we were carrying M16s but many times when we swept villages, and I promise you always respectfully, the villagers invited us to share tea. And we did. I really liked them and still do. I shared tea today. It's a big, big deal here.

Binh Phuoc was a routine. The only way I knew it was Monday was that the medics went around Mondays giving us our malaria pills. Otherwise, every day was the same: up at daylight, breakfast, check out vehicles (my truck had 10 tires and usually 1 or 2 were flat), fix any issues (i.e., backbreaking labor repairing tires) and go out and fight the war.

3MAR70, Tuesday

The first day of training at the Go Devil Academy started with a welcome by the Academy commander. He welcomed us to the 9th Infantry Division and to Vietnam. He answered the "big question," what was all of this "Go Devil" business about? He explained that the 9th Division was under General Patton's command during his World War II drive into the heart of Germany. And, while witnessing a 9th Division armored unit drive straight up the middle of an opposing German armored force, he was quoted as exclaiming, "Look at those Go Devils go." We were expected to uphold the tradition. Before turning us over to an instructor, he repeated a saying I would hear many times during the months ahead, "Killing is our business, and business has been good."

We went outside to some bleachers for a class in map reading. I was an Eagle Scout, had my private pilot license and had extensive map reading during my Advanced Individual Training (AIT) in armor at Fort Knox. I could have taught the class. I pissed off the sergeant/instructor because I knew all the answers. But he was impressed that a dumb E-2 private really knew exactly what he was talking about. He knew, and I knew, that this kind of skill could mean the difference between life and death. We broke for lunch and went right back to school.

The afternoon session was on booby traps. This subject had everybody's attention. After over 6 years of nightly TV newscasts, daily newspaper reports, and the grief of neighbors who had lost sons there, Vietnam was not an unknown subject. Few men of draft age were oblivious to the more germane realities; among those most commonly discussed were the reports of various booby traps. Our Go Devil Academy instructor loved his subject.

Many of the devices we were told about involved explosives. There were grenades with the pins tied to tripwires; if you tripped the wire, the pin was pulled, and the grenade went off. A more devious device was a tripwire hooked to a detonator designed to explode when the wire, once tripped, was relaxed. The difference was that with the standard tripwire, hooked to a delayed charge (e.g., a grenade), there was a little time to get away from the charge once you realized what had happened. With the tension fuse, it was all over. There were pressure mines that exploded when stepped upon. There were command-detonated mines (command dets) that were wired to a detonator held by an enemy troop who would hide 50 to 100 feet away in the jungle. He could wait and blow the mine on the target of his choice. There were rifle rounds rigged and buried so that, when stepped on, the primer was driven onto a nail and the round discharged, in this case blowing a hole in your foot (toe poppers). There were endless variations.

The more sinister variations were passive. There were boards with sharpened spikes. These were buried to await a wrong step that would drive the spikes through a foot. Our boots had metal plates in the soles to protect against this hazard. This was little comfort. There were concealed pits full of sharpened stakes waiting to pierce muscles and guts. And, whether spike or stake, they both were smeared with feces to insure a devastating infection. The Vietcong (alias "V.C.," "Victor Charlie," "Charlie" or, when deserved, which was too often, "Sir Charles") were in it to win. Go Devil Academy told it all; they even had a demonstration booby trap course. I learned a lot today, but it didn't make me feel any better. Before I went to bed, to await my guard shift, I wrote home for the first time.

Reflections on Vietnam

Journal Entry, March 25, 2016

I crossed the border into Cambodia and left Vietnam today, technically for the 4th time: the 1st when my Army unit moved into Cambodia in 1970, the 2nd when the same year I went to Hawaii for R&R and the 3rd when I caught my "freedom bird" back to the World 46 years ago. I doubt that I will ever return. Would love to but just too far and I'm not getting any younger. But I have been reflecting on this visit.

Imagine your 50th high school reunion in reverse. I attended my class-of-1964 Milby High School reunion year before last. Big deal. Lots of old, old friends. Also, lots of gray, extra pounds and a little less spring in our step. Now, imagine that reunion in reverse. When I left Vietnam 46 years ago (South Vietnam to be clear), it was in shambles and heading for collapse and defeat. The U.S. could only do so much. But when I walked into this 2016 Vietnam reunion the attendees were young, vibrant and building a new, modern, economically sound country. The government is communist and many of the people don't like some of the policies. But the results are positive and plain to see. On balance, Vietnam's communist government may be functioning better than ours.

The other thing I've been thinking about is what this visit meant to me. Imagine that a long time ago you were reading the only copy of the most vivid novel you ever read. And just as you got to the last chapter you lost the book. For the next 46 years you've wondered how the story ended. Then one day you find the book and are able to read that last chapter. And it's the best ending you could possibly have imagined. With a peaceful sense of satisfaction, you close the book and put it back on the shelf.

*Ray W. Luce receives the Army Commendation Medal,
Tan An, Vietnam.*

The Cambodian Killing Fields

Journal Entry, March 26, 2016

I visited the Cambodian "Killing Fields" today. This tragedy was real and occurred during my lifetime. So, I believe it's worth cataloging and commenting on.

At the entrance to the Killing Fields there's a foreboding, maybe like entering Auschwitz. As you move closer to the main memorial structure, you're unsure what's in store. At the entrance, your emotions are stunned. And as you enter and witness the Khmer Rouge carnage, it numbs all sensibility. As I walked around the area surrounding the main memorial structure, I noticed that bone fragments continue to literally bubble out of the ground. After visiting the Killing Fields, I visited a nearby school turned prison, which processed these poor souls to their final fate. And I visited privately with a Killing Fields survivor. His wife was not so fortunate. Through an interpreter, he told me his story of survival.

The Khmer Rouge controlled Cambodia from 1975-1979. It was a brutal regime created by Pol Pot. At the outset the cities were emptied and by the end 2,000,000 out of 8,000,000 innocent people were murdered; the worst genocide since WWII.

By 1979 the Vietnamese next door had had enough of the brutality. The world knew what was occurring there and the Vietnamese, good and decent people, had the only army in the area that could respond. They did and liberated the Cambodian people from an unspeakable nightmare. I've always admired them for that. And they left Cambodia 10 years later in 1989. They obviously had no territorial ambitions and the result was the beautiful, peaceful current-day Cambodia I am experiencing.

Pol Pot (1925-1998) studied in Paris 1947-1953 and returned to Cambodia a communist. Ho Chi Minh (1890-1969) studied in Paris 1919-1923 and returned to Vietnam a communist. But Pol Pot became a monster while Ho Chi Minh became the George Washington of his country. Why the difference is unknowable.

A movie, *The Killing Fields*, was made in 1984. I recommend it to those who are interested in what happened there.

The Killing Fields main memorial structure.

There are no words to describe entering the main Killing Fields memorial.

A Small School in a Remote Cambodian Village

Journal Entry, March 27, 2016

This was the highlight of the day. In the afternoon our riverboat nudged into the shore and put down a gangplank onto the Mekong bank. We walked to a small village and ran into a tiny outdoor school. It's Sunday, so no class. But the teacher was there tutoring a couple of girl students in math. The best part was the teacher took a few minutes to talk to the small group of folks I was traveling with. Amazingly, he was a survivor of Pol Pot's Khmer Rouge genocide.

During those terrible years, from 1975 to 1979, he had to pose as an uneducated worker. If the Khmer Rouge figured out that he was an educated man, he would have been immediately executed; probably tortured. Brutality beyond comprehension. He's 82 now and teaches math in this small village where he was born. When I saw the math examples he had on the blackboard, these little girls enthusiastic about their books, and thought about how fortunate we are to live in such a bountiful country, I could hardly hold back the tears.

Some of the group, through an interpreter, asked questions of the teacher about his life under Pol Pot. I wanted to ask him whether he knew about the American invasion of Cambodia in 1970 and, if he did, what did he think about it. But I was afraid I wouldn't like the answer, so I didn't ask.

Sunday tutoring in outdoor school in small Cambodian village.

Epilogue

"Let every nation know, whether it wishes us well or ill, that we shall pay any price, bear any burden, meet any hardship, support any friend, oppose any foe to assure the survival and the success of liberty."

JOHN F. KENNEDY, JANUARY 20, 1961

LATER IN HIS presidency, John Kennedy would challenge us to put a man on the moon and return him safely to earth by the end of the decade. It is ironic, and perhaps a fitting perspective, to realize that it was easier to achieve the lunar challenge than to succeed in Vietnam. It is difficult to imagine how any people could focus simultaneously on two such disparate goals. And of the two, the failure haunts us still.

Veterans Day 2016

The election is over. Some are happy. Some are not. Some are in the streets. But today most paused to reflect on our veterans. Just under one half of one percent of the population currently serves in the military. Just over 10 percent of living

Americans have served in the military. To quote Churchill, "Never in the field of human conflict was so much owed by so many to so few."

I began the day representing my Missouri City, Texas, VFW Post 4010 at the Quail Valley Rotary Club annual veterans' recognition luncheon. There were about a hundred folks there, half veterans, some Rotary member vets, but mostly guest vets. Veterans from every conflict were represented, except Operation Urgent Fury in Granada 1983 and Operation Just Cause in Panama 1989. Five WWII vets were there with their helpers: all over 90, the oldest 97, a female WAC who served on Eisenhower's staff in the European theater. Vets love their headgear and most vets had their black baseball caps on festooned with pins.

The program began with the presentation of the colors by the Dulles High School Army ROTC. Then a retired officer said the prayer. He was black and in the mold of Martin Luther King. We've all been at events where prayers are offered, often perfunctorily. But as I listened, head bowed, and eyes closed, I began to realize this man was pronouncing a powerful message of faith and hope. I don't think I'll go to hell for opening my eyes and looking around the room. Lots of tears on cheeks. I had forgotten the power of prayer: for the nation, for our veterans, and for our souls. Worth the price of admission, if the program ended there. But much more to come.

Next the Rotary MC went from table to table with the mike asking vets to stand and state name, rank, service (e.g., army, navy, etc.) and where served. As I mentioned, WWII, Korea, Vietnam, Desert Storm, Desert Shield, Iraq, and Afghanistan vets were represented. I guess we are a militaristic nation. Many vets offered a few thoughts on their service, and the impact of hearing seventy-plus years of struggle to protect our heritage as Americans was humbling. Lots of resolve and courage concentrated in that room.

Our speaker was an army colonel, commander of an armor battalion in Desert Storm. He spoke about all the NCOs (sergeants) that shaped him during his military career. For those of you who weren't in the military, NCOs are the military's version of middle management that most of us spend our lives working for in corporate America. I was an armored crewman so, after lunch, I took a moment to visit with him. His tanks were a little more modern than the ones I trained on. And lunch was over.

My take away was that I'm sure that some version of what I recounted to you above took place all over America today— a great Veterans Day.

CPSIA information can be obtained
at www.ICGtesting.com
Printed in the USA
LVHW03s1059060818
586103LV00022B/582/P